CHEAP HOTELS

CHEAP HOTELS

Daisann McLane

TASCHEN

KÖLN LONDON MADRID NEW YORK PARIS TOKYO

Front cover: Hotel Lord, Sao Luís, Brazil

© 2002 TASCHEN GmbH

Hohenzollernring 53, D-50672 Köln

www.taschen.com

© 2002 by Daisann McLane

Edited by Allison Arieff

Design by Bryan Burkhart / MODERNHOUSE

French translation by Philippe Safavi, Paris

German translation by Clara Drechsler, Cologne

Printed in Germany

ISBN 3–8228–1440–7

LIJIANG MICROWAVE HOTEL
LIJIANG, YUNNAN, CHINA

CONTENTS

PRICE LIST

$ 45.00 AROKO BUNGALOWS, COOK ISLANDS	$ 87.00 HOTEL DUE TORRI, ROME
$ 54.00 HOTEL PANAMONTE, PANAMA	$ 89.00 ADAMS HOUSE BED AND BREAKFAST INN, TEXAS
$ 54.00 HOTEL BELLEVUE, CROATIA	$ 95.00 DEER RUN BED AND BREAKFAST, FLORIDA
$ 55.00 RYOKAN SHIGETSU, TOKYO	$ 98.00 PEACE AND PLENTY INN, NEW ZEALAND
$ 55.00 SS NADSON JEANE, BRAZIL	$ 99.00 SHIPPEN WAY INN, PHILADELPHIA
$ 55.00 HOTEL PARÍS, MADRID	$ 99.00 ROBIN'S NEST BED AND BREAKFAST, TEXAS
$ 57.00 BEST WESTERN MANAUS, BRAZIL	$ 99.00 THE PAINTED LADY INN, TEXAS
$ 58.00 HOTEL ZLATOROG, SLOVENIA	$ 99.00 HOTEL WOLCOTT, NEW YORK
$ 58.00 HOTEL TERME PREISTORICHE, PADOVA	$ 99.00 THE NEW YORKER HOTEL, NEW YORK
$ 60.00 HOTEL CASTELAR, BUENOS AIRES	$ 99.00 HOTEL DEL SOL, SAN FRANCISCO
$ 60.00 HOTEL LA FONDA, MEXICO	$ 100.00 OVER LOOK LODGE, BRAZIL
$ 60.00 TINGUM VILLAGE INTERNATIONAL HOTEL, BAHAMAS	$ 102.00 MOTEL 6, CHICAGO
$ 65.00 SOMATHEERAM AYURVEDIC BEACH RESORT, INDIA	$ 107.00 SORAT ART'OTEL, BERLIN
$ 65.00 SANAFIR HOTEL, EGYPT	$ 112.00 PASO ROBLES INN, CALIFORNIA
$ 67.00 HOTEL KÜNSTLERHEIM LUISE, BERLIN	$ 115.00 THE BARNACLE BED AND BREAKFAST, FLORIDA
$ 67.50 MARINA INN, SAN FRANCISCO	$ 125.00 ON THE AVE HOTEL, NEW YORK
$ 69.00 OHANA EDGEWATER, HAWAII	$ 125.00 DEETJEN'S BIG SUR INN, CALIFORNIA
$ 70.00 THE TONGAN BEACH RESORT, TONGA	$ 125.00 PARK BROMPTON INN, CHICAGO
$ 75.00 BISHOP LEI INTERNATIONAL HOUSE, HONG KONG	$ 128.00 ASTON AT THE EXECUTIVE CENTRE HOTEL, HAWAII
$ 75.00 SHOJOSHIN-IN MONASTERY, JAPAN	$ 129.00 HOTEL GEORGE, WASHINGTON D.C.
$ 75.00 CASA VERARDO, VENICE	$ 135.00 HOTEL SOFITEL, TOKYO
$ 75.00 TABARD INN, WASHINGTON D.C.	$ 185.00 WHITE SULPHUR SPRINGS RESORT AND SPA, CALIFORNIA
$ 79.00 CAPRI MOTEL, CALIFORNIA	
$ 82.00 SHANGRI-LA, KUALA LUMPUR	
$ 82.00 HOTEL EUROPA, FLORENCE	
$ 83.00 HOTEL DE FILOSOOF, AMSTERDAM	
$ 85.00 THE ANDREWS HOTEL, SAN FRANCISCO	
$ 87.00 HOTEL ALESSANDRA, FLORENCE	

INTRODUCTION

LA NOUVELLE DÉFINITION DE VOTRE VIE COMMENCE À PRA ARTHIT MANSION

Le centre de la ville qui
Rendra votre vie heureuse
Tout l'instant que vous pensez.

—BROCHURE, PRA ARTHIT MANSION, BANGKOK

Aucune chambre d'hôtel n'a encore changé ma vie, mais beaucoup d'entre elles m'ont rendue, de manière inattendue et inexplicable, heureuse. Je ne parle pas des suites somptueuses, minutieusement conçues et déco-rées, qui ornent les pages promotionnelles des magazines de voyage. Depuis que j'ai accepté la mission, il y a quatre ans, de rédiger une rubrique sur les voyages à petit budget dans un journal, j'ai passé la nuit dans plus de 200 chambres différentes. Cependant, aucune n'avait sa fontaine d'eau potable, son service de chambre 24 heures sur 24, ni même ses authentiques déesses Khmers en pierre enchâssées dans le carrelage de la salle de bains.

Pourtant, dans des espaces si exigus que, une fois allongée, je pouvais toucher les murs de part et d'autre, dans des lits recouverts de couvertures en polyester, j'ai parfois connu un vrai confort et une paix profonde.

Je ne doute pas qu'il soit possible de s'offrir la béatitude hôtelière – à partir de 1000 dollars la nuit, l'hôtel a intérêt à offrir le nec plus ultra – mais j'ai découvert que, lorsqu'on descend en dessous de ce que les agences de voyages qualifient de catégorie «super luxe», il n'y a plus de corrélation entre le prix d'une chambre d'hôtel et le plaisir qu'elle vous procure. Cela s'explique en partie par les différences de cours des devises dans l'économie mondiale. J'ai payé 102 dollars la nuit au Motel 6 au cœur de Chicago, Illinois, et 500 bath (environ 12,50 dollars) la nuit à la Peachy Guest House, au centre de Bangkok. Les deux chambres avaient la même taille et, plus ou moins, les mêmes équipements.

INTRODUCTION

EINLEITUNG

THE NEW DEFINITION IN YOUR LIFE STARTS FROM PRA ARTHIT MANSION

**The center of the city which will
Make your life happy all the
Moment that you expect.**

—BROCHURE, PRA ARTHIT MANSION, BANGKOK

DIE NEUE DEFINITION IHRES LEBENS BEGINNT AM PRA ARTHIT MANSION

**Dem Mittelpunkt der Stadt,
Der Ihr Leben beglücken wird
In allen Momenten, die Sie erwarten.**

—BROSCHÜRE, PRA ARTHIT MANSION, BANGKOK

No hotel room has yet changed my life, but many of them have made me, unexpectedly and inexplicably, happy. I am not talking about the fantastic, painstakingly designed and realized chambers that decorate the pages of high-end travel magazines. Since I took an assignment, four years ago, to write a newspaper column about traveling on a budget, I have stayed overnight in more than 200 different rooms. However not a single one has had a private fountain, 24-hour butler service, or authentic Khmer stone goddesses embedded in the bathroom tile.

And yet, in spaces so tiny I can reach out while sleeping and touch both walls, in beds draped with pilled polyester covers, I have experienced great comfort, and profound peace.

While I believe it is possible to buy your way to hotel room bliss—at $1,000 a night, plus, a hotel had better deliver ultimate satisfaction—I've found that once you drop below what travel agents call the "super-luxury" category, there's often no correlation between a hotel room's price and the pleasure it delivers. Part of this has to do with the unevenness of currency values in the global economy. I paid $102 for a night at the Motel 6 in downtown Chicago, Illinois, and 500 bhat (about $12.50) for a night at the Peachy Guest House in downtown Bangkok. Both rooms were the same size and offered, more or less, the same amenities.

But in the Motel 6 depression blanketed me every time I entered my room and hit a cloud of American chain-hotel odor, an assault of industrial carpet polycar-

Kein Hotelzimmer hat bisher mein Leben verändert, aber viele von ihnen haben mich in unerwarteter und undefinierbarer Weise beglückt. Ich spreche hier nicht von den fantastischen, minutiös designten und ausgestalteten Gemächern, wie sie die Hochglanzseiten edlerer Reisemagazine zieren. Seit ich vor vier Jahren die Aufgabe übernommen habe, eine Zeitungskolumne über Reisen mit kleinem Budget zu schreiben, habe ich in mehr als 200 verschiedenen Zimmern übernachtet. Und keines davon hatte einen eigenen Springbrunnen, 24-Stunden-Zimmerservice oder Badezimmerkacheln, in die authentische Steinskulpturen von Khmer-Göttinnen eingelassen waren.

Und doch habe ich in Zimmern, die so winzig waren, dass ich beide Wände berühren konnte, wenn ich im Schlaf die Arme ausstreckte, und in Betten mit fusseligen Tagesdecken aus Polyester wunderbaren Komfort und tiefen Frieden erfahren.

Ich bin durchaus der Meinung, dass Hotelzimmerseligkeit für Geld zu haben ist – ab 1000 Dollar die Nacht aufwärts sollte ein Hotel gefälligst für unüberbietbares Wohlbefinden sorgen –, doch wenn man einmal unter die Kategorie sinkt, die Reisebüros als „super luxury" bezeichnen, sagt der Preis eines Hotelzimmers, wie ich festgestellt habe, oft nichts darüber aus, welche Annehmlichkeiten es bietet. Das hängt zum Teil mit der unterschiedlichen Kaufkraft der verschiedenen Währungen zusammen. Ich habe schon 102 Dollar für eine Übernachtung im Motel 6 im Zentrum von Chicago, Illinois, gezahlt und 500 Bhat (etwa 12,50 Dollar) für eine

Cependant, au Motel 6, la déprime s'abattait sur moi chaque fois que j'entrais dans ma chambre et me retrouvais enveloppée par un nuage d'odeur de chaîne hôtelière américaine, un assaut de moquette industrielle pure plastique et de désodorisant floral synthétique. Pourquoi tous les hôtels bon marché aux Etats-Unis sentent-ils toujours la voiture neuve? Quelle est la véritable odeur de Chicago? Je ne le saurai jamais. D'un autre côté, à la Peachy Guest House, une ouverture avec un étrange motif en fer forgé genre Miami Beach revu et corrigé à l'orientale séparait ma chambre de ma salle de bains, source de fascination sans fin. En flânant suffisamment longtemps dans Bangkok, finirais-je par découvrir un jour tout un quartier Art Déco Thaï? Dans la salle de bains, tous les soirs à minuit, un caméléon jaune pâle à trois pattes sortait de derrière la cuvette des w.-c. Le matin, il avait disparu. Je pense encore à lui.

Ce sont souvent les détails les plus inattendus qui déclenchent mes désirs d'hôtel.

Le linge, par exemple. La plupart des gens reviennent d'Italie en s'extasiant sur sa cuisine. Je suis rentrée de mon premier voyage en Italie avec une passion irrémédiable pour les serviettes italiennes. Les salles de bains des hôtels italiens, mêmes les moins chers où j'ai séjourné, avaient toutes des serviettes en lin d'un blanc immaculé suspendues près du lavabo, de la douche, même du bidet. Dans quelques endroits, comme à l'Hotel Terme Preistoriche à Montegrotto Terme, elles étaient posées sur un porte-serviettes chauffant chromé et équipé d'un thermostat. Elevée dans le tissu éponge américain, rien ne m'avait préparée à cette rencontre avec le vieux monde civilisé. Certes, mes chambres italiennes à 65 dollars la nuit avaient généralement la taille de la penderie de l'une de ces chambres parfumées au plastique du Motel 6 de Chicago, mais ne préféreriez-vous

bons and synthetic floral disinfectant. Why must every cheap hotel in America smell like a new car? What did Chicago actually smell like? Mysteries to me, forever. The Peachy Guest House room, on the other hand, had a window with a curious iron Oriental Miami Beach motif separating the bedroom from the bathroom, a source of endless fascination. If I poked around Bangkok long enough would I suddenly stumble upon an entire neighborhood of Thai Art-Deco? In the bathroom, every night at midnight, a tiny pale-yellow chameleon with three legs emerged from behind the toilet. By morning he was always gone. I still think about him.

The strangest things can push the buttons of my hotel desire.

Linens, for instance. Most people come home from Italy raving about the food; I came home from my first trip to Italy with a permanent crush on Italian towels. Italian hotel bathrooms, even in the inexpensive places in which I was staying, all had spotless white linens, hanging beside the sink, the shower, even the bidet. In a few places, like the Hotel Terme Preistoriche in Montegrotto Terme, they were draped over a chrome rack heater with a temperature control. Raised on American terrycloth, I was unprepared for this encounter with the civilized Old World. True, my $65-a-night rooms in Italy were usually the size of a closet in one of those polycarbon-scented chambers at the Chicago Motel 6. But wouldn't you rather live in a closet wrapped in starched, ironed—and heated!—linen towels?

It delights me that Italians make fine linens a priority in their hotels, even the cheap ones. All around the world, each culture holds fast to its own version of hotel room comfort, and to the little detail that it would be unthinkable to overlook, even in the humblest lodging. In Japan, it is the teapot on the lacquer tray, beside a lacquer cup and a container of green tea. In the Amazon, it

Nacht im Peachy Guest House im Zentrum von Bangkok. Beide Zimmer hatten die gleiche Größe und boten mehr oder weniger den gleichen Komfort.

Aber im Motel 6 überkamen mich jedes Mal Depressionen, wenn ich mein Zimmer betrat und von amerikanischem Hotelkettengeruch empfangen wurde, diesem aus Synthetikausdünstungen der Teppichböden und Desinfektionsmitteln mit künstlichem Blumenduft zusammengemischten Anschlag auf die Geruchsnerven. Warum muss jedes preiswerte Hotel in Amerika wie ein neu gekauftes Auto riechen? Wie riecht Chicago wohl in Wirklichkeit? Beides werde ich wohl nie erfahren. Mein Zimmer im Peachy Guest House hingegen hatte ein schmiedeeisernes Fenster mit einem eigenartigen Orient-trifft-Miami-Beach-Motiv zwischen Schlafraum und Bad – ein unerschöpflicher Quell der Faszination. Würde ich auf ein komplettes Viertel in Thai-Art-déco stoßen, wenn ich nur lange genug durch Bangkok streifte? Im Badezimmer tauchte jede Nacht um Mitternacht ein winziges, blassgelbes Chamäleon mit drei Beinen hinter der Toilette auf. Morgens war es stets verschwunden. Ich denke heute noch an das kleine Kerlchen.

Die seltsamsten Dinge können meine Hotelsehnsüchte wecken.

Wäsche zum Beispiel. Die meisten Menschen kommen aus Italien zurück und schwärmen vom Essen; ich kehrte von meinem ersten Italienbesuch mit einer bleibenden Begeisterung für italienische Handtücher heim. In den Badezimmern der italienischen Hotels, selbst der preiswerten Häuser, in denen ich abstieg, hingen überall blütenweiße Handtücher neben dem Waschbecken, der Dusche und selbst dem Bidet. In manchen Häusern, etwa dem Hotel Terme Preistoriche in Montegrotto Terme, hingen sie über einem heizbaren, verchromten Handtuchhalter mit eigenem Temperaturregler. Aufgewachsen mit amerikanischem Frottee, war ich auf diese Begegnung

pas vivre dans une penderie enveloppée dans des serviettes en lin amidonnées, repassées et chauffées?

Je suis ravie que les Italiens fassent du beau linge
une des priorités de leurs hôtels, quel que soit leur stan-
ding. Partout dans le monde, chaque culture s'accroche
à sa propre conception du confort hôtelier et aux petits
détails qu'il serait inconcevable de négliger même dans
les lieux les plus humbles. Au Japon, c'est la théière
sur son plateau laqué, posée près d'une tasse laquée
et d'une boîte de thé vert. En Amazonie, ce sont les
puissants crochets en métal fichés dans deux murs se
faisant face afin que chacun puisse y accrocher son
hamac pour la siesta de l'après-midi (la faire dans un
vrai lit serait déplacé). En Thaïlande, il y a toujours une
maison miniature quelque part dans l'hôtel, avec de
petits personnages en plastique et des bâtons d'encens
se consumant, une ruse thaï pour attirer tous les esprits
traînant dans le coin dans cette maison de poupée afin
qu'ils n'errent pas dans les couloirs et dérangent votre
séjour. Dans les petits hôtels du sud du Pacifique, tous
les matins après avoir fait le ménage, les femmes de
chambre déposent une fleur de frangipanier ou de gin-
gembre sur votre oreiller. Celle-ci se flétrit lentement
dans la chaleur de la journée, remplissant la pièce de
son parfum capiteux. A Bali, les femmes de ménage
murmurent une courte prière et déposent de mystérieux
petits paquets faits de riz, de fleurs et d'épices envelop-
pés dans une feuille de bananier sur le seuil de votre
porte.

Aujourd'hui encore, on trouve facilement des hôtels
présentant ce genre de touches de grâce, qui vous en
apprennent autant sur une localité donnée que n'importe
quel guide. Mais je crains que cela ne dure pas. Le tourisme international est un secteur d'activité d'une am-
pleur vertigineuse. Selon un groupe d'analystes, en
2001, il a représenté 10,7 pour cent du produit intérieur

is the strong metal hooks on opposite walls, for hanging your own hammock during the afternoon siesta (when a bed mattress just wouldn't be right). In Thailand, always, there's a miniature house somewhere on the hotel premises, with little plastic people in it, and incense burning— a Thai trick to coax all the local spirits into the doll's house, so they won't roam the corridors and disturb your stay. The housekeepers in South Pacific guest houses will lay frangipani or ginger blossoms on your pillow every morning after they clean the room, that wilt slowly in the heat of the day, filling the air with intoxicating fragrance. The housekeepers in Bali whisper a little prayer and place tiny mysterious packets of rice, flowers, and spices wrapped in a banana leaf, on your doorstep.

Finding hotels with grace notes like these, which tell you as much about a given locality as any guidebook, is not a difficult thing right now. But I fear that may change. World tourism is a staggeringly big business. According to one group of analysts, in 2001 it accounted for 10.7 percent of the global gross domestic product, or one in every 12.2 jobs in the world. And its scope increases with each passing year. As tourism globalizes, private hotels melt into the arms of multi-national corporations, which prioritize standardization over individuality, consistency over quirkiness. While I have spent enough nights in sad, decrepit rooms to appreciate the joy of a familiar hotel chain every now and then, I fret about what may happen to the spirit houses, the wilted fragripani, the stiffly creased hand towel by the bidet.

I also worry about the philosophy that seems to be shaping the new boutique hotels that are currently popping up as alternatives to the chains in hip Western capital cities. The guru of these design-intensive lodgings, hotelier Ian Schrager, once proclaimed, "You are where you sleep, because where you sleep says to the world, 'This is who I am'." Yet a world in which the only

mit der zivilisierten Alten Welt nicht vorbereitet. Zugegeben, meine 65-Dollar-die-Nacht-Zimmer in Italien waren in der Regel so groß wie die Wandschränke der nach Kunststoff riechenden Zimmer im Motel 6 in Chicago. Aber wer würde es nicht vorziehen, in einem Wandschrank zu wohnen, dafür aber in gestärkte, gebügelte – und angewärmte! – Leinenhandtücher gehüllt?

Ich kann mich dafür begeistern, dass die Italiener in ihren Hotels, selbst in den preiswerten, feiner Leinenwäsche oberste Priorität einräumen. Jede Kultur der Welt hält an ihrer ureigenen Version von Hotelzimmerkomfort und an Kleinigkeiten fest, die zu vergessen undenkbar wäre, selbst in den bescheidensten Unterkünften. In Japan ist es die Teekanne auf dem lackierten Tablett, neben einer lackierten Tasse und einer Dose mit grünem Tee. Am Amazonas sind es die starken Metallhaken an einander gegenüberliegenden Wänden, an denen man während der nachmittäglichen Siesta – zu der eine simple Bettmatratze einfach nicht passen würde – seine persönliche Hängematte einhängen kann. In Thailand findet sich stets irgendwo auf dem Hotelgelände ein Miniaturhaus mit kleinen Plastikfiguren und brennendem Weihrauch darin – ein Thai-Trick, um alle Geister am Ort in das Puppenhaus zu locken, damit sie nicht auf den Fluren herumspuken und den Aufenthalt der Gäste stören. Die Zimmermädchen in den Pensionen im Süd-Pazifik legen jeden Morgen, nachdem sie das Zimmer geputzt haben, Jasmin- oder Ingwerblüten aufs Kopfkissen, die in der Tageshitze langsam welken und einen betörenden Duft verströmen. Die Zimmermädchen in Bali flüstern ein kurzes Gebet und legen kleine, geheimnisvolle, in ein Bananenblatt eingeschlagene Päckchen mit Reis, Blumen und Gewürzen auf die Schwelle.

Im Moment ist es nicht schwierig, Hotels mit solch liebenswerten Eigenarten zu finden, Hotels, die mehr

Quand les chambres d'hôtels sont parfaites, j'ai tendance à oublier les détails.

brut mondial, ainsi qu'un emploi sur 12,2 dans le monde. Sa portée s'étend chaque année. A mesure que le tourisme se mondialise, les hôtels privés sont absorbés par des multinationales qui privilégient la standardisation sur l'individualité, la consistance sur l'originalité. Si j'ai passé suffisamment de nuits dans des chambres tristes et décrépites pour pouvoir apprécier de temps à autre le confort familier d'une chaîne hôtelière, je me demande bien ce qu'il va arriver aux maisons aux esprits, aux fleurs de frangipaniers fanées, aux serviettes de main plissées avec art près du bidet.

Je m'inquiète également de la philosophie derrière les nouveaux hôtels-boutiques qui surgissent çà et là dans les capitales branchées d'Occident comme une alternative aux chaînes. L'hôtelier Ian Schrager, gourou de ces établissements très orientés design, a proclamé: «Dites-moi où vous dormez et je vous dirai qui vous êtes, car l'endroit où vous dormez dit au reste du monde: ‹Voilà qui je suis.›» Un monde où la seule alternative à la chaîne hôtelière est un dortoir décoratif pour obsédés de la mode ne m'attire pas beaucoup.

A New York, je dors déjà dans un endroit qui dit «Voilà qui je suis»: mon appartement. Quand je voyage, je cherche autre chose, pas une habitation qui reflète une version imaginaire de moi-même, mais une chambre qui me parle, d'une manière ou d'une autre, des gens chez qui je suis.

Quand je rentre dans une chambre d'hôtel, quelle qu'elle soit, je commence par ouvrir les stores ou les rideaux. La chambre est ma première fenêtre sur un nouvel endroit, sur une culture que ne connais pas encore, et je tiens à en voir le plus possible. L'hôtel cairote al-Hussein, dans le vieux quartier de Khan el-Khalili, avait des draps tachés et des moutons de poussière dans les coins, mais il avait également un petit balcon surplombant la plus grande et la plus belle mosquée de

When hotel rooms are perfect, I often forget the details.

Wenn Hotelzimmer perfekt sind, entfallen mir oft die Details.

über einen Ort verraten als jeder Reiseführer. Aber ich fürchte, das könnte sich ändern. Weltweiter Tourismus ist ein ungeheuerer Wirtschaftsfaktor. Untersuchungen zufolge entfielen darauf im Jahr 2001 10,7 Prozent des weltweiten Bruttoinlandsprodukts, oder anders gesagt, der Tourismus sicherte einen von 12,2 Arbeitsplätzen auf der Welt. Und sein Umfang nimmt von Jahr zu Jahr zu. Während sich der Tourismus globalisiert, geraten privat geführte Hotels in die Klauen internationaler Konzerne, die Standardisierung über Individualität und Einheitlichkeit über Einfallsreichtum stellen. Ich habe genug Nächte in trostlosen, schäbigen Zimmern verbracht, um dann und wann die Vorzüge einer vertrauten Hotelkette schätzen zu können, aber mich quält die Frage, was aus den Geisterhäusern, dem welkenden Jasmin und den sauber gefalteten Handtüchern neben dem Bidet werden wird.

Ebenso viele Sorgen macht mir die neue Philosophie, nach der offenbar die neuen Boutique-Hotels gestaltet werden, die gegenwärtig als Alternativen zu den Hotels der großen Ketten in hippen westlichen Metropolen aus dem Boden schießen. Der Guru solcher designlastigen Unterkünfte, Hotelier Ian Schrager, hat verkündet: „Sagen Sie mir, wo Sie schlafen und ich sage Ihnen, wer Sie sind, denn der Ort wo Sie schlafen, sagt der Welt, ‚So bin ich.'" Eine Welt, in der die einzige Alternative zur Übernachtung in Häusern der Hotelketten das Absteigen in Lifestyle-Herbergen ist, klingt mir nicht gerade verlockend.

In New York City schlafe ich bereits an einem Ort, der sagt: „So bin ich." Dieser Ort ist meine Wohnung. Aber wenn ich auf Reisen bin, suche ich nach etwas anderem. Nicht nach einem Zimmer, das irgendeine Fantasieversion meiner selbst widerspiegelt, sondern ein Zimmer, das mir durch irgendeine Kleinigkeit etwas über die Menschen erzählt, die ich besuche.

21

la ville. J'y ai pris une chambre. Au Broadlands Lodging House de Madras, devant les volets en bois ouverts de ma single à quatre dollars, draps et serviettes non fournis, défilaient des processions nuptiales menée par des trompettistes et des éléphants parés de bijoux. Les parades, les processions religieuses, les gongs, les chants rythmiques et les étranges cris d'animaux ont tous, à un moment ou un autre de mes voyages, enrichi mon expérience des chambres d'hôtels.

Parfois, comme dans le cas de la «Chambre Liberace» du Painted Lady Inn de San Antonio, la fenêtre de ma chambre ne donne sur rien de plus intéressant qu'une ruelle. Mais quand la chambre donnant sur la ruelle est ornée de lustres et de portraits de Liberace dans des cadres dorés, qui songerait à s'en plaindre à la direction?

Une fois, lors d'un séjour à Kuala Lumpur en Malaisie, j'ai dormi dans une vraie chambre de luxe. Les devises asiatiques s'effondraient et le gouvernement malaysien avait gelé le ringitt, qui, en quelques semaines, avait perdu près de 40 pour cent de sa valeur par rapport au dollar. Profitant de l'occasion, je pris une chambre au Shangri-La (existe-t-il un nom plus idyllique pour une chaîne hôtelière?) pour 82 dollars, soit moins que dans un Quality Inn à Houston.

Naturellement, la chambre était une perfection de baignoire en marbre et de robinetterie dorée, de meubles damassés, d'orchidées fraîches sur la table de nuit. A moins que ce ne soit des lys. Quand les chambres d'hôtels sont parfaites, j'ai tendance à oublier les détails.

En revanche, voici ce sont je me souviens: une forêt de squelettes d'acier, de béton et de grues figées sur place devant ma fenêtre panoramique au 14e étage. En Malaisie, le «tigre» de l'économie s'était étranglé soudain en plein rugissement. Grâce à cette chambre, ce que m'avaient appris les gros titres abstraits de la

alternative to staying in a chain hotel is to stay in life-style dormitories for the style-obsessed doesn't sound like much fun to me.

In New York City, I already sleep in a place that says, "This is who I am." That place is my apartment. But when traveling, I am looking for something else. Not a room that reflects some fantasy version of me, but one that tells me, in some small way, about the people I'm visiting.

The first thing I do when I enter any hotel room for the first time is open all the shades and curtains. The room is my first window on a new place, an unexplored culture, and I want to make sure I can see as much as possible. The Hotel al-Hussein, in Cairo's old Khan el-Khalili district, had stained sheets and dust balls—but it also had a little balcony overlooking the city's largest and most splendid mosque. I checked in. Outside my four-dollar, no-sheets-or-towels single at the Broadlands Lodging House in Madras, wedding parades led by trumpeters and jewel-bedecked elephants drifted past my open wooden shutters. Parades, religious processions, clanging gongs, rhythmic chants and unexplained animal noises have all, at one time or another, enriched my hotel room experience.

Sometimes, as in the case of the "Liberace Room" at San Antonio's Painted Lady Inn, my hotel room window looks out on nothing more interesting than a side alley. But when alley-facing rooms are dripping in chandeliers and hung with gold-framed portraits of Liberace, how can you complain to the management?

Once on a trip to Kuala Lumpur, Malaysia, I got to stay in a bona-fide luxury hotel room. Asian currencies were collapsing, and the Malaysian government had frozen the ringgit, which was suddenly worth about 40-percent less dollars than it had been a few weeks before. Seizing the instant, I booked a room at the Shangri-

Wenn ich ein Hotelzimmer zum ersten Mal betrete, öffne ich sofort alle Jalousien und Vorhänge. Von meinem Zimmer werfe ich den ersten Blick auf einen neuen Ort, eine unerforschte Kultur, und ich möchte sicher sein, so viel wie möglich zu sehen. Im Hotel al-Hussein in Kairos altem Khan el-Khalili-Viertel gab es schmutzige Laken und Staubflocken, aber dafür hatte mein Zimmer einen kleinen Balkon, von dem aus man auf die großartigste Moschee der Stadt hinunterblickte. Ich checkte ein. Draußen vor meinem Vier-Dollar-Einzelzimmer ohne Bettzeug und Handtücher im Broadlands Lodging House in Madras zogen von Trompetern und juwelengeschmückten Elefanten angeführte Hochzeitsparaden unter meinen geöffneten Fensterläden aus Holz vorbei. Umzüge, religiöse Prozessionen, hallende Gongs, rhythmische Gesänge und rätselhafte Tierlaute haben alle irgendwann einmal meine Hotelzimmererfahrung bereichert.

Manchmal, wie im Falle des „Liberace-Zimmers" im Painted Lady Inn in San Antonio, sah ich aus meinem Hotelzimmerfenster nichts Interessanteres als eine Gasse. Aber wer wird sich schon bei der Hotelleitung beschweren, wenn die gassenseitigen Zimmer im Glanz von Kronleuchtern und goldgerahmten Liberace-Porträts erstrahlen?

Einmal, auf einem Trip nach Kuala Lumpur in Malaysia, landete ich in einem echten Luxushotelzimmer. Die asiatischen Währungen kollabierten gerade, und die malaysische Regierung hatte den Kurs des Ringitt eingefroren, der nun schlagartig rund 40 Prozent weniger Dollars wert war als noch ein paar Wochen zuvor. Ich packte die Gelegenheit beim Schopf und buchte ein Zimmer im Shangri-La – kann es einen perfekteren Namen für eine Hotelkette geben? – für 82 Dollar, das heißt zu einem günstigeren Preis als im Quality Inn in Houston.

presse était désormais visible et concret. Oh, et je me rappelle une autre chose, une affichette sur le réfrigérateur disant: «Les clients sont priés de ne pas apporter des durians dans la chambre.»

Ce n'est peut-être pas le genre de souvenir qu'on s'attend à rapporter du paradis terrestre, mais c'est l'un de mes meilleurs.

La (could a hotel chain have a more perfect name?) for $82—less than the price of a Quality Inn in Houston.

The room, of course, was a perfection of marble tubs and gilded faucets, gold damask upholstery, and fresh orchids on the nightstand. Actually, they might have been lilies. When hotel rooms are perfect, I often forget the details.

Here's what I do remember: A forest of steel building skeletons and construction cranes frozen motionless outside my 14th-story picture window. In Malaysia, the "tiger" economy had stopped, abruptly, in mid-roar. Thanks to the room, what I had understood from abstract headlines was now visible and concrete. Oh, and I remember one other thing—a sign, on the refrigerator, that said, "Guests are requested to not bring Durian fruit into the room."

Perhaps this is not the kind of memory one expects to carry home from Shangri-La. But it is among the best of mine.

Das Zimmer war selbstredend der Inbegriff aller Perfektion mit marmornen Bädern und vergoldeten Wasserhähnen, goldenen Damastpolstern und frischen Orchideen auf dem Nachttisch. Es könnten auch Lilien gewesen sein. Wenn Hotelzimmer perfekt sind, entfallen mir oft die Details.

An eins erinnere ich mich noch: einen bewegungslos eingefrorenen Wald aus stählernen Baugerüsten und Baukränen vor meinem Fenster im 14. Stock. In Malaysia war die „Tiger"-Wirtschaft mitten im Sprung zum Erliegen gekommen. Dank meines Zimmers war das, was ich abstrakten Schlagzeilen entnommen hatte, nun sichtbar und konkret. Oh, und ich erinnere mich noch an ein anderes Detail – das Schild auf dem Kühlschrank: „Die Gäste werden gebeten, keine Durian-Früchte mit aufs Zimmer zu bringen."

Vielleicht ist das nicht die Art von Erinnerungen, die man aus dem Shangri-La mit nach Hause zu nehmen erwartet. Aber sie zählen zu meinen besten.

31

LES FORMALITÉS

Au moment de l'arrivée, mon rythme cardiaque s'accélère. Arriver dans un hôtel pour la première fois, c'est un peu comme de se rendre à un rendez-vous galant avec un parfait inconnu. J'ai beau glaner au préalable toutes les informations possibles dans les guides ou auprès d'autres voyageurs, je ne sais jamais à l'avance si je serais charmée, indifférente ou malheureuse en pénétrant dans le hall.

Si ma réservation figure bien dans le registre, je me détends un peu. Parmi les autres bons présages: du personnel en uniforme dans l'entrée, des clients souriants, des bouquets frais, un cocktail de bienvenue. Les mauvais augures: un comptoir d'accueil protégé par une vitre pare-balles, le personnel portant des badges disant: «Bonjour, mon nom est …» et des animaux domestiqués. (Sauf s'il s'agit de pachydermes. Il existe un hôtel au sud de l'Inde célèbre pour son éléphant qui traverse la réception tous les matins en route vers le temple voisin. C'est considéré comme un signe de grande chance.)

Suit le rituel de la signature du registre. Dans certaines parties du monde, les hôtels ne s'embarrassent plus de cette formalité, dans d'autres, on vous tend un formulaire sur lequel vous devez indiquer le détail de votre itinéraire, vos projets d'avenir et votre curriculum vitae en lettres capitales sur une carte de 8 x 12 cm. Puis arrive le moment de vérité: on vous conduit à «la chambre». A moins qu'on vous tende une clef et qu'on vous envoie dans la nuit noire armée d'une lampe torche.

Je préfère porter moi-même mes bagages. J'aime être seule quand je pénètre dans la chambre pour la première fois. La présence d'un groom rôdant autour de moi fausse mon radar et je risque de ne pas remarquer tout de suite la dépression en U au milieu du lit ou la fenêtre donnant sur un conduit d'aération.

THE DRILL

GRUNDKENNTNISSE

At the moment of arrival, my heart begins to flutter. Checking into an unfamiliar hotel is a little like going on a blind date. No matter how much advance information I've been able to gather from guidebooks or from other travelers, I can't predict if I will be happy, indifferent or miserable until I step into the lobby.

If my reservation is on the books, I relax a little. Other good omens: uniformed employees in the lobby, smiling guests, fresh flowers, a welcome cocktail. Bad omens: bulletproof protective glass around the check-in desk, employees wearing badges that say, "Have a Nice Day My Name Is ..." and domesticated animals. (With the exception of elephants. There's a hotel in South India that is famous for its elephant, which visits the lobby every morning on its way to a nearby temple. This is considered to be very good luck.)

The ritual of signing in follows. In some parts of the world, hotels no longer bother with this; in others, you're handed a form that requests you to list your entire itinerary, your future plans, and your curriculum vitae in block letters on a 3 x 5 card. And then the moment of truth: you are led to The Room. Or given a key and sent off into the dark night with a flashlight.

I prefer carrying my own bag. I like to be alone when I step into a room for the first time; the presence of a hovering bellhop throws my radar off, and I end up not noticing the u-shaped depression in the center of the bed, or the airshaft-facing window.

Tip the bellhop, open the windows, unpack. Take off shoes. Play with the knobs on the mysterious box by the bed—is it a radio? A heater? Toss Balinese sarong over hideous bedspread. Investigate nooks and crannies. Joy is a small refrigerator that works. A pretty clay teapot with a container of green tea leaves and a thermos of boiling water in a Japanese ryokan. A mint condition Art Deco sink in Manhattan. In the tropics, a fluttering ceiling

Im Augenblick meiner Ankunft beginnt mein Herz nervös zu flattern. In ein noch unbekanntes Hotel einzuchecken, hat was von einem Blind Date. Egal, wie viele Informationen aus Reiseführern oder von anderen Reisenden ich vorher zusammentragen konnte, ehe ich nicht die Lobby betreten habe, kann ich nicht voraussagen, ob die Erfahrung zufriedenstellend, ambivalent oder trist ausfallen wird.

Wenn meine Reservierung im Gästebuch steht, entspanne ich mich ein wenig. Andere gute Omen sind: uniformierte Angestellte in der Lobby, lächelnde Gäste, frische Blumen, ein Begrüßungscocktail. Schlechte Vorzeichen: kugelsicheres Glas um den Empfangstisch, Angestellte, die Schildchen mit der Aufschrift „Einen schönen Tag, mein Name ist ..." tragen, und zahme Tiere. (Mit Ausnahme von Elefanten. In Südindien gibt es ein Hotel, dass für seinen Elefanten berühmt ist, der jeden Morgen auf dem Weg zum nahen Tempel die Lobby besucht. Das wird als großes Glück betrachtet.)

Es folgt das Ritual des Sicheintragens. In manchen Teilen der Welt legen Hotels keinen Wert mehr darauf, in anderen bekommt man ein Formular ausgehändigt, das einen auffordert, seine gesamte Reiseroute, seine Pläne für die Zukunft und seinen Lebenslauf in Blockbuchstaben auf eine streichholzschachtelgroße Karte zu schreiben. Und dann der Moment der Wahrheit: Man wird zu „dem Zimmer" geführt. Oder bekommt einen Schlüssel ausgehändigt und wird mit einer Taschenlampe in die finstere Nacht geschickt.

Ich ziehe es vor, meine Reisetasche selber zu tragen. Ich bin gerne allein, wenn ich ein Zimmer zum ersten Mal betrete. Die Anwesenheit eines herumstehenden Pagen blockiert mein Radar, und am Ende übersehe ich noch die U-förmige Vertiefung in der Bettmitte oder das auf einen Wetterschacht hinausgehende Fenster.

Donner un pourboire au chasseur, ouvrir les fenêtres, défaire sa valise. Enlever ses chaussures. Tripoter les boutons de la boîte mystérieuse à côté du lit … est-ce une radio? Un radiateur? Jeter un sarong balinais sur le couvre-lit hideux. Inspecter les moindres coins et recoins. Le bonheur, c'est un petit réfrigérateur qui fonctionne. Une jolie théière en terre cuite avec une boîte de feuilles de thé vert et un thermos d'eau bouillante dans un ryokan japonais. Un lavabo Art Déco en parfait état à Manhattan. Sous les tropiques, un ventilateur de plafond tournoyant doucement. Le cauchemar, c'est une chambre rose chewing-gum éclairée par des ampoules fluorescentes bon marché. De mystérieuses taches brunes sur les murs. Des draps troués, en Inde.

Je règle la petite antenne sur le poste de télévision et déchiffre les caractères cyrilliques ou chinois sur la télécommande. En appuyant au hasard, je trouve deux chaînes, chacune diffusant le même bulletin d'information dans une langue que je comprends à peine. Oh oh … il y a une carte couverte de lignes sinueuses et un présentateur montrant un point en répétant encore et encore un mot qui ressemble à «typhon». Il est temps de descendre prendre un verre au bar. Si c'est vraiment mon jour de chance, il y aura peut-être une piscine et j'aurai même le temps de piquer une tête avant le déluge.

fan. Misery is a bubble gum-pink room lit entirely by cheap florescent bulbs. Mysterious brown stains on the walls. Bedsheets with holes, in India.

I adjust the rabbit ears on the television and decipher the Cyrillic or Chinese characters on the remote. By randomly pressing buttons, I find two stations, each broadcasting the same newscast in a language I can barely make out. Uh oh ... there's a map covered with wavy lines, and a newscaster pointing to a spot and speaking, over and over, a word that sounds like "typhoon." Time to go downstairs and have a drink. If I'm really on a roll, there will be a pool, and enough time for a swim before the deluge.

Dem Pagen ein Trinkgeld geben, die Fenster öffnen und auspacken. Die Schuhe ausziehen. Mit den Knöpfen an der geheimnisvollen Kiste neben dem Bett spielen. Ist das ein Radio? Ein Heizlüfter? Den balinesischen Sarong über die abscheuliche Tagesdecke werfen. Glück ist ein kleiner Kühlschrank, der funktioniert. Die hübsche, tönerne Teekanne, die Dose mit grünem Tee und die Thermosflasche mit kochend heißem Wasser in einem japanischen Ryokan. Ein tadellos erhaltenes Art-déco-Waschbecken in Manhattan. Ein sich drehender Deckenventilator in den Tropen. Tristesse ist ein ganz in Kaugummirosa gehaltenes Zimmer, das ausschließlich von billigen Neonröhren beleuchtet wird. Ominöse braune Flecken an den Wänden. Bettlaken mit Löchern in Indien.

Ich knicke die Hasenohren der Zimmerantenne auf dem Fernseher zurecht und entziffere die kyrillischen oder chinesischen Schriftzeichen auf der Fernbedienung. Indem ich wahllos auf die Knöpfe drücke, finde ich zwei Sender, die beide dieselben Nachrichten in einer Sprache bringen, die ich kaum verstehen kann. Oho-oho ... da ist eine mit Wellenlinien bedeckte Landkarte, und der Nachrichtensprecher zeigt auf einen Punkt und wiederholt immerzu ein Wort, das wie „Taifun" klingt. Zeit, nach unten zu gehen und einen Drink zu nehmen. Wenn mein Glück anhält, gibt es einen Pool, und mir bleibt vor der Sintflut noch genügend Zeit zum Schwimmen.

Arriver dans un hôtel pour la première fois est un peu comme de se rendre à un rendez-vous galant avec un parfait inconnu. J'ai beau glaner au préalable toutes les informations possibles dans les guides ou auprès d'autres voyageurs, je ne sais jamais à l'avance si je serais charmée, indifférente ou malheureuse en pénétrant dans le hall.

Checking into an unfamiliar hotel is a little like going on a blind date. No matter how much advance information I've been able to gather from guidebooks or from other travelers, I can't predict if I will be happy, indifferent or miserable until I step into the lobby.

In ein noch unbekanntes Hotel einzuchecken, hat was von einem Blind Date. Egal, wie viele Informationen aus Reiseführern oder von anderen Reisenden ich vorher zusammentragen konnte, ehe ich nicht die Lobby betreten habe, kann ich nicht voraussagen, ob die Erfahrung zufriedenstellend, ambivalent oder trist ausfallen wird.

L'ATTAQUE DES DESSUS-DE-LIT QUI TUENT

Ils ont des noms: Captiva, Vanessa, Sussex, Ikat, Royal Manor et New Jamestown. Je les ai découverts sur l'Internet un après-midi, cherchant à percer un mystère qui me laisse perplexe depuis des années. Pourquoi tous les hôtels économiques des Etats-Unis ont les mêmes cinq imprimés affreux?

D'accord, j'exagère un peu. Il y a plus de cinq modèles hideux qui circulent dans le secteur du dessus-de-lit. Peut-être une vingtaine ou une trentaine. Mais qui peut bien être responsable de ces horreurs aux couleurs criardes tourbillonnantes, de ces malheureuses taches de Rorschach, de cette profusion de palmiers et de roses de jardin?

Comme je l'avais toujours soupçonné, la prolifération de ces couvre-lits en polyester à l'échelle nationale est une affaire de sous. Aux Etats-Unis, il existe plusieurs grands fabriquants de textiles et de literie spécialisés dans le secteur hôtelier. Dans la plupart des villes américaines, vous ne pouvez pas mettre n'importe quelle couverture sur un lit, il faut que celle-ci soit conforme aux normes anti-incendie. Le polyester doit donc être fortement ignifugé et enduit d'une couche protectrice qui rappelle la texture de la toile cirée.

Ensuite, il y a les frais de blanchisserie, déjà une lourde charge pour n'importe quel établissement mais, pour un hôtel économique, un véritable puits sans fond. Plus vous descendez dans la chaîne hôtelière, plus on regarde à la dépense. Un jour, un journaliste du *Des Moines Register* a contacté plusieurs hôtels locaux et leur a demandé combien de temps ils laissaient passer entre deux lavages. «Au West des Moines Marriott, la direction affirme changer les dessus-de-lit toutes les six semaines. Au Motel 6 de Des Moines, ils sont lavés une fois par trimestre, à moins qu'ils ne présentent des taches ‹visibles›.»

Il faudrait un technicien de la police scientifique

ATTACK OF THE KILLER BEDSPREADS

ANGRIFF DER KILLER-TAGESDECKEN

They have names: Captiva, Vanessa, Sussex, Ikat, Royal Manor and New Jamestown. I discovered this on the Internet one afternoon, in search of a clue to a mystery that has puzzled me for years. Why do all budget American hotel rooms have the same five ugly patterns?

Okay, I'm exaggerating. There are more than five hideous patterns circulating in the Bedspread Industry. Maybe twenty or thirty. But just who is responsible for these atrocities of clashing, swirling colors, these unfortunate Rorschach splotches, these profusions of cabbage roses and palm trees?

As I've always suspected, the national proliferation of ugly polyester-filled covers has its roots in the proverbial bottom line. In the United States, there are several large textile and bedding manufacturers catering to the needs of the hotel industry. In most American cities, you can't put just any blanket on a bed—it has to meet the local fire code standards. Hence, the polyester so heavily coated and treated with flame retardant that it feels like plastic bubble wrap.

Then there's laundry—for any hotel, a big expense, but for budget hotels, a crippling one. As you work your way down the hotel chain, it's an expense that gets pinched. A reporter for the *Des Moines Register* once called a few local hotels and asked them how long they waited in-between washings. "At the West Des Moines Marriott, management says the bedspreads are changed every six weeks," he was told. "At the Motel 6 in Des Moines, bedspreads are laundered every three months unless there is a 'visible' stain."

It would take a forensic expert to separate the design from the stains on Captiva, Vanessa, Sussex, Ikat or Royal Manor.

I try not to think about such things as I pull down the garish coverlet and brace myself for another night in a cheap motel. I can deal with the aesthetic attack that

Sie haben Namen: Captiva, Vanessa, Sussex, Ikat, Royal Manor und New Jamestown. Das entdeckte ich eines Nachmittags im Internet, als ich einem Rätsel nachspürte, das mich schon lange beschäftigte: Warum finden sich in allen preiswerten Hotelzimmern in den USA die gleichen fünf hässlichen Muster?

Na gut, ich übertreibe. In der Tagesdecken-Industrie kursieren mehr als fünf scheußliche Muster. Vielleicht 20 oder 30. Aber wer ist bloß verantwortlich für diese Gräueltaten von sich beißenden Farben, diese unglückseligen Rorschachtest-Kleckse, diesen unerschöpflichen Reichtum an gefüllten Rosen und Palmen?

Wie ich schon immer vermutete, ist der landesweite Vormarsch hässlicher, polyestergefüllter Decken eine Kostenfrage. In den Vereinigten Staaten gibt es mehrere Textil- und Bettwäschehersteller, die die Hotelindustrie beliefern. In den meisten amerikanischen Städten darf man nicht einfach eine x-beliebige Decke auf das Hotelbett legen – sie muss den örtlichen Brandschutzvorschriften genügen. Daher wird das Polyester so kräftig mit feuerhemmenden Mitteln beschichtet und behandelt, dass es sich wie Luftpolsterfolie anfühlt.

Dann ist da noch die Reinigung, für jedes Hotel ein hoher, für preisgünstige Hotels jedoch erdrückender Kostenfaktor. Je weiter man sich die Hotelkategorien hinunterarbeitet, desto lieber wird an dieser Ausgabe gespart. Ein Reporter des *Des Moines Register* hat einmal verschiedene Hotels am Ort angerufen und nach den Intervallen gefragt, in denen die Tagesdecken gewechselt und gewaschen würden. Im West Des Moines Marriott, teilte ihm die Geschäftsführung mit, würden die Tagesdecken alle sechs Wochen gewechselt. Im Motel 6 in Des Moines kommen die Tagesdecken alle drei Monate in die Wäsche, es sei denn, sie hätten „sichtbare" Flecken.

Um bei Captiva, Vanessa, Sussex, Ikat oder Royal

pour pouvoir distinguer les motifs des taches sur Captiva, Vanessa, Sussex, Ikat ou Royal Manor.

J'essaye de ne pas penser à ce genre de choses quand j'enlève le couvre-lit tape à l'œil et rassemble mon courage avant une nouvelle nuit dans un hôtel bon marché. Je peux affronter l'agression esthétique d'un dessus-de-lit infâme, mais je supporte moins bien l'idée que ce dernier, au cours de la dernière semaine de son trimestre de service, pourrait également m'attaquer au niveau moléculaire.

a horrific bedspread provokes, but I can't handle the thought that my bedspread, in the last week of its three-month shift, may attack me at the molecular level, too.

Manor etwaige Flecken vom Muster zu trennen, bedürfte es schon eines erfahrenen Forensikers.

Ich versuche, nicht an solche Dinge zu denken, wenn ich die schreiend bunte Decke herunterziehe und mich für eine weitere Nacht in einem preiswerten Hotel wappne. Mit dem ästhetischen Anschlag in Gestalt einer grauenhaften Tagesdecke kann ich umgehen, aber nicht mit der Vorstellung, dass meine Decke mich in der letzten Woche ihrer Drei-Monats-Schicht auch noch auf molekularer Ebene angreifen könnte ...

AVENTURES AU PARADIS

Les photos qui suivent capturent un moment particulier
dans le cycle des vie de beaux endroits: des moments
que j'aime à considérer comme «des hôtels au paradis».
C'est le début de la découverte d'une destination par
le secteur du tourisme. Les gros investisseurs multina-
tionaux et leurs grands projets hôteliers n'en sont pas
encore là, mais les petits hôtels bon marché et les pen-
sions de famille commencent à disparaître. Surgissent
alors dans le paysage des constructions qui se situent
quelque part entre les deux, le plus souvent des bâti-
ments construits à la hâte qui ont peu à voir avec la
culture pour laquelle vous avez parcouru tout ce chemin.
Vous savez que vous êtes tombé sur un paradis en
phase de transition quand vous regardez le mur de
votre chambre et pouvez compter les parpaings. Bien
que ces hôtels fonctionnels et rectangulaires soient
souvent sans charme, ils ont aussi beaucoup d'aspects
attachants. Dans les phases préliminaires du développe-
ment touristique, les blocs de béton font généralement
leur première apparition dans les hôtels familiaux les
plus sympathiques et ambitieux. Dans le Tiers-Monde,
ils représentent la modernité, la propreté et font la fierté
du lieu. La Posada Tupiulandia à Alter do Chao, une
minuscule station balnéaire brésilienne nichée autour
de la seule plage de sable blanc de l'Amazone, est un
classique «Paradis de Béton de la première heure».
Naturellement, c'est le seul hôtel de la ville avec une
climatisation qui fonctionne.

    Qu'arrive-t-il à ces hôtels modestes une fois que le
tourisme local décolle? Parfois, ils survivent, légèrement
fanés, la vue depuis leurs balcons obstruée par des
hôtels plus grands, plus clinquants et plus modernes. Ils
vieillissent, deviennent émouvants. Le Edgewater, l'un
de la demi-douzaine de vétérans construits à Honolulu
dans les années 1950 et 1960 lors du premier essor
hôtelier de Waikiki Beach, a désormais une allure funky

ADVENTURES IN PARADISE

ABENTEUER IM PARADIES

The following snapshots capture a particular moment in the life cycle of beautiful places: the moment I like to think of as "Hotels In Paradise". This is the beginning of a destination's discovery by the tourist trade. Big multinational investors and their expensive resort developments are still off in a distant future, but the cheap, family-run guesthouses and hostels are dwindling away. What appears on the landscape are lodgings that fall somewhere between the two—typically, quickly constructed buildings with little connection to the culture that you've come all the way here to discover. You know when you've hit a paradise in transition mode if you can look at your hotel room wall and count the cinderblocks. Though these functional, rectangular hotels can be charmless, there's still a lot to like about them. In the beginning stages of tourist development, concrete blocks usually make their debut in the nicest, most ambitious of the family-run hotels. In the Third World, they represent modernity, cleanliness, and pride of place. The Posada Tupiulandia in Alter do Chao, a tiny Brazilian resort that sits on the Amazon River's only white sand beach, is classic Early Concrete Paradise. Naturally, it's the only guesthouse in town with air conditioning that works.

What happens to these modest hotels as local tourism evolves? Sometimes they survive, a little faded, their balcony views obstructed by larger, glitzier, more modern hotels. They age, they become poignant. The Edgewater, one of a half-dozen Honolulu dowagers built in the 50s and 60s, during the first tourist boom in Waikiki Beach, now has a funky, faded Elvis Presley era allure. La Fonda, with its uneven floors and ramshackle, thrift shop furniture, is a throwback to the days when Hollywood's bad-boy actors and directors ran off to spend wild weekends on Mexico's windblown Baja Peninsula.

Die folgenden Schnappschüsse halten einen ganz speziellen Moment im Lebenszyklus schöner Orte fest: den Moment, den ich in Gedanken gerne „Hotels im Paradies" nenne. Damit meine ich die Anfänge der Entdeckung eines Reiseziels durch die Touristikindustrie. Große internationale Investoren und ihre teuren Ferienanlagen sind noch ferne Zukunft, aber die preiswerten, als Familienbetrieb geführten Pensionen und Hotels sind bereits auf dem Rückzug. Die jetzt auf der Bildfläche erscheinenden Unterkünfte fallen irgendwo dazwischen – im typischen Fall schnell hochgezogene Gebäude, die wenig mit der Kultur verbindet, die zu entdecken man hergekommen ist. Man weiß, dass man ein Paradies im Wandel erwischt hat, wenn man an seine Hotelzimmerwand blickt und die Schlackenbetonsteine zählen kann. Auch wenn diese funktionalen, rechtwinkligen Hotels reizlos sein können, gibt es doch vieles, das man an ihnen mögen kann. In den Anfangsstadien touristischer Erschließung machen Betonblöcke ihr Debüt in den nettesten und ambitioniertesten der Hotels im Familienbetrieb. In der Dritten Welt stehen sie für Modernität, Sauberkeit und Besitzerstolz. Die Posada Tupiulandia in Alter do Chao, einem winzigen brasilianischen Ferienort am einzigen weißen Sandstrand des Amazonas, ist ein klassisches frühes Betonparadies. Und selbstredend die einzige Pension in der Stadt mit funktionierender Klmaanlage.

Was geschieht mit diesen bescheidenen Hotels, wenn sich der örtliche Tourismus entwickelt? Manchmal überleben sie, ein bisschen verblasst, die Aussichten von den Balkonen durch höhere, schickere und modernere Hotels versperrt. Sie altern, sie werden prägnanter. Das Edgewater, eine von einem halben Dutzend ehrwürdigen Matronen, die in den 1950ern und 1960ern während des ersten Touristikbooms am Waikiki Beach in Honolulu errichtet wurden, hat nun den abgefahrenen,

71

désuète à la Elvis Presley. La Fonda, avec ses planchers irréguliers et ses meubles d'occasion délabrés, rappelle les jours lointains où les acteurs et metteurs en scène d'Hollywood venaient s'encanailler pendant des week-ends de débauche sur la Baja Peninsula venteuse du Mexique.

Inconsolable, je déballe mon barda dans le Maina Sunset Motel à Aitutaki, un atoll isolé des îles Cook. Les meubles en contreplaqué et acier de ma chambre semblent sortis d'un vieux catalogue d'IKEA et, dans la cour, la piscine empestant le chlore ressemble à n'importe quelle piscine d'un motel en bordure de nationale aux Etats-Unis. J'ai beau chercher la moindre trace du sud du Pacifique, je n'en trouve aucune, à l'exception des orchidées imprimées sur le dessus-de-lit.

Puis, à quelques pas de ma porte, le voilà: un lagon d'un bleu somptueux. Les nuages au-dessus de ma tête se transforment en filets rose vif et mandarine. Je m'assois sur la plage, observant le spectacle magique, jusqu'à l'arrivée d'un escadron de moustiques. Je bats en retraite dans ma chambre, me retranchant derrière les moustiquaires. La climatisation fonctionne et le pommeau de douche déverse de l'eau chaude en abondance. Ça aussi, c'est le paradis.

I unpack my gear in the Maina Sunset Motel in Aitutaki, a remote atoll in the Cook Islands. I am inconsolable. The plywood and steel furniture in my room looks like vintage IKEA, and in the courtyard there's a chlorine-scented swimming pool no different from any pool in an American highway motel. Searching carefully for any trace of the South Pacific I find none, unless you count the orchid print on the bedspread.

But steps from my door, here it is: a gorgeous blue lagoon, now turning violet at dusk. The clouds above transform into streaks of fiery pink and tangerine. I sit on the beach, watching this magic unfold—until a squadron of mosquitoes arrives. And then I flee to my room, where the windows are well-screened, the air conditioning works, and abundant hot water gushes from the shower head. This, too, is paradise.

verblassten Charme der Elvis-Presley-Ära. Das La Fonda mit seinen unebenen Böden und seinem wackeligen Trödel-Mobiliar versetzt einen in die Zeiten zurück, als die Schurkendarsteller und Regisseure Hollywoods ausbüxten, um wilde Wochenenden auf der windzerzausten mexikanischen Baja Peninsula zu verbringen.

Ich packe meine Sachen im Maina Sunset Motel auf Aitutaki aus, einem Atoll der Cook Islands. Ich bin untröstlich. Das Mobiliar aus Sperrholz und Stahl in meinem Zimmer sieht nach IKEA aus, und im Hof ist ein chlorgeschwängerter Pool, der sich in nichts vom Pool eines amerikanischen Highway-Motels unterscheidet. Obwohl ich akribisch nach der kleinsten Spur von Südsee suche, finde ich nichts, es sei denn, man zählt das Orchideenmuster auf der Tagesdecke mit.

Aber nur wenige Schritte von meiner Tür ist sie: eine prächtige blaue Lagune, die sich jetzt in der Dämmerung violett färbt. Die Wolken am Himmel verwandeln sich in glühend pink- und leuchtend orangefarbene Streifen. Ich sitze am Strand und schaue zu, wie sich dieser Zauber entfaltet, bis ein Geschwader von Moskitos eintrifft. Dann fliehe ich in mein Zimmer, wo die Fenster gut abgedichtet sind, die Klimaanlage läuft und reichlich heißes Wasser aus dem Duschkopf sprudelt. Auch das ist das Paradies.

Je bats en retraite dans ma chambre, me retranchant derrière les moustiquaires. La climatisation fonctionne et le pommeau de douche déverse de
l'eau chaude en abondance. Ça aussi, c'est le paradis.

I flee to my room, where the windows are well-screened, the air conditioning works, and abundant hot water gushes from the shower head.

Dann fliehe ich in mein Zimmer, wo die Fenster gut abgedichtet sind,
die Klimaanlage läuft und reichlich heißes Wasser aus dem Duschkopf
sprudelt. Auch das ist das Paradies.

LES AVATARS DU MINIMALISME

Au cours des années 1990, l'industrie hôtelière a eu la révélation du Modernisme. Soudain, pratiquement toutes les villes cosmopolites avaient leur «hôtel-boutique», où le personnel, sélectionné par une agence de casting, accueillait des hordes de voyageurs branchés dans des chambres dépouillées de tout meuble superflu et décorées principalement de différentes nuances de blanc. Equipés d'accessoires astucieux et d'éléments de salles de bains design en acier brossé créés par de célèbres architectes et décorateurs, ces hôtels attiraient une classe de jeunes voyageurs nouveaux riches trop occupés à admirer les abat-jour ingénieux et les écritoires intégrés pour remarquer qu'il y avait tout juste assez de place dans leur chambre hors de prix pour faire le tour du lit.

Le petit secret bien gardé de ces hôtels-boutiques était le suivant: le Modernisme est une affaire rentable. Les Japonais n'ont pas attendu cette révélation pour savoir qu'en réduisant une chambre d'hôtel au minimum, en évitant tous les détails inutiles, vous pouvez loger des gens confortablement dans des espaces très réduits. Or, plus l'espace par occupant est petit, plus la marge de profit est grande.

J'ai observé cette tendance se développer sur quelques années, de loin car le prix à payer pour ce Néo-minimalisme dépassait nettement mon budget de voyage. Puis, vers la fin de la décennie, les inévitables ersatz ont commencé à apparaître. J'ai d'abord remarqué que, dans beaucoup d'hôtels bon marché rénovés depuis peu, la palette de couleur s'était réduite à divers tons de gris, de blancs et de noirs. Enfin, vers 1999, j'ai pris une chambre dans un hôtel économique de Manhattan qui venait d'être refait, suis entrée dans la salle de bain et ai vu un lavabo conique en acier. J'ai su alors que le Mini-malisme s'était infiltré dans les masses.

Personnellement, à la fin d'une journée chargée, je préfère me retrouver entre quatre murs blancs et nus

TRICKLE-DOWN MINIMALISM

DAS ERBE DES MINIMALISMUS

During the 1990s, the hotel industry discovered Modernism in a big way. Suddenly, in just about every international city, there was a "boutique hotel", where the employees, chosen by casting agents, welcomed throngs of trend setters to rooms bare of excess furniture and decorated mainly in shades of white. Outfitted with clever accessories and sleek, brushed stainless steel bathroom fixtures created by famous architects and interior designers, these hotels grabbed the attention of a young, new monied class of travelers, mostly too busy admiring the clever lampshades and built-in desks to notice that there was barely enough space in their pricey hotel room to walk around the bed.

The unspoken little business secret of these boutique hotels was this: Modernism can be very cost-effective. The Japanese have known for years that if you pare a hotel room down to the basics, and avoid fussy details, you can make people comfortable in very small spaces. And the smaller the space per guest, the higher the profit margin.

I watched this trend develop over a few years, from afar, since the price tag on the New Minimalist rooms was too high for my travel budget. But then, late in the decade, the inevitable knockoffs began to appear on the scene. First I noticed that in many recently renovated cheap hotels the color palette had shrunk to shades of gray, black and white. Then, around 1999, I checked into a just-renovated budget hotel in Manhattan, walked into its bathroom and beheld a cone-shaped, steel sink. I knew that Minimalism had trickled-down to the masses.

Personally, I prefer coming back at the end of the day to clean bare walls, rather than calico wallpaper—much more relaxing. On the other hand, I don't enjoy spending the first hour of my hotel stay searching like a bloodhound for the light switch (hint: they're often on the telephone console) and then figuring out how to make

In den 1990er Jahren entdeckte die Hotelbranche im großen Stil den Modernismus. Plötzlich gab es in praktisch jeder internationalen Großstadt ein „Boutique-Hotel", in dem das von Casting-Agenturen ausgesuchte Personal Heerscharen von Trendsettern in Zimmern willkommen hieß, die jedes überflüssigen Möbels entbehrten und vornehmlich in Weißtönen gehalten waren. Ausgestattet mit cleveren Accessoires und todschicken Badezimmerinstallationen aus gebürstetem Edelstahl, entworfen von berühmten Architekten und Innenarchitekten, fanden diese Hotels Anklang bei einer jungen, frisch zu Geld gekommenen Schicht von Reisenden, die meistens zu sehr damit beschäftigt waren, die raffinierten Lampenschirme und integrierten Schreibpulte zu bewundern, um zu bemerken, dass ihr kostspieliges Hotelzimmer kaum genug Platz bot, um einmal ums Bett zu gehen.

Das kleine Geschäftsgeheimnis solcher Boutique-Hotels war Folgendes: Modernismus kann sehr kostensparend sein. Die Japaner wussten seit Jahren, dass man Menschen auch in sehr kleinen Hotelzimmern sehr komfortabel unterbringen kann, sofern man sich auf das Allernotwendigste beschränkt und verspielte Details weglässt. Je weniger Raum pro Gast, desto höher die Profitspanne.

Ich habe die Entwicklung dieses Trends über mehrere Jahre beobachtet. Allerdings aus der Ferne, da das Preisschild an den neo-minimalistischen Zimmern für mein Reisebudget zu hoch war. Aber dann, gegen Ende des Jahrzehnts, erschienen die unvermeidlichen Billigkopien auf der Szene. Zuerst entdeckte ich, dass in vielen frisch renovierten Hotels die Farbpalette auf Schwarz, Weiß und diverse Graustufen zusammengeschrumpft war. Dann, ungefähr 1999, checkte ich in ein gerade renoviertes, preiswertes Hotel in Manhattan ein, ging ins Badezimmer und erblickte ein kegelförmiges Wasch-

que cernée par un papier peint en imitation calicot, c'est
nettement plus relaxant. D'un autre côté, je n'aime pas
passer ma première heure dans une nouvelle chambre
d'hôtel à traquer l'interrupteur comme un limier (un indi-
ce: ils sont souvent au-dessus de la console télépho-
nique) puis à essayer de comprendre comment il fonctionne. S'il faut un point décisif pour départager ces
deux tendances, ce doit être celui-ci: dans les hôtels
avec des murs blancs et nus (contrairement à ceux avec
papier peint imprimé), il y a presque toujours du bon
café bien fort.

them work. If there's a tiebreaker in this dilemma, it is this: In hotels with bare walls (unlike the ones with calico wallpaper), there is almost always a supply of good, strong coffee.

becken aus Edelstahl. Da wusste ich, dass der Minimalismus beim gemeinen Volk angekommen war.

Ich selbst kehre am Ende eines Tages lieber zu kahlen Wänden als zu Streublümchen-Tapeten zurück – das ist viel entspannender. Allerdings suche ich in der ersten Stunde meines Hotelaufenthalts nicht gerne wie ein Bluthund nach dem Lichtschalter (kleiner Tipp: sie finden sich oft an der Telefonkonsole), um dann noch rauskriegen zu müssen, wie er funktioniert. Wenn es eines gibt, das in diesem Dilemma weiterhilft, ist es folgende Erwägung: In Hotels mit kahlen Wänden bekommt man – anders als in denen mit Blümchentapete – fast immer einen guten, starken Kaffee.

Manager,

(   ).

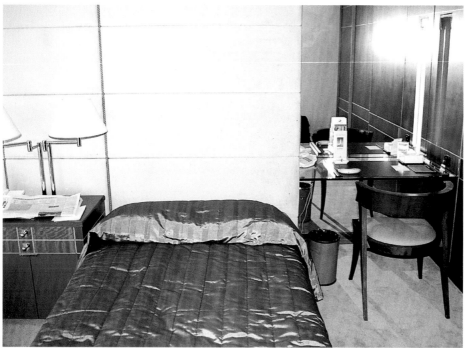

LE SOMMEIL

Certaines chambres d'hôtels vous charment par leur vue ou leur décoration, d'autres s'attardent dans votre mémoire du fait de leur site ou de leur atmosphère. Mais il en est des rares et des spéciales qui vous offrent le plaisir d'un sommeil profond et satisfaisant.

Les hôtels où j'ai le mieux dormi ont tous un point commun: de beaux draps en coton blanc uni. Ils sont souvent amidonnés et repassés. Ils portent parfois le nom de l'hôtel amoureusement brodé sur l'ourlet supérieur. Dans de nombreux cas, ils sont vieux mais leurs parties élimées ont été soigneusement raccommodées à la main dans un réseau de minuscules points blancs.

Je suis convaincue que le sommeil est compromis par les mélanges de polyester.

Outre une literie adéquate, la chambre peut favoriser une relaxation totale de différentes manières: si l'hôtel se trouve en ville, un double vitrage, voire triple, est nécessaire pour réduire le bruit de la rue à un murmure. S'il se trouve à la campagne, il vaut mieux que ce soit dans un endroit où les coqs sont proscrits. Sous les tropiques, et dans certaines régions tempérées, les meilleurs amis du sommeil sont un ventilateur de plafond tournant en douceur et une ample moustiquaire (vérifier toujours qu'il n'y a pas de trous dans le voilage et apporter une boîte de pansements avec vous pour les colmater le cas échéant). Au Moyen-Orient ou en Inde, choisissez l'hôtel le plus éloigné de la mosquée locale, à moins de vouloir être réveillé de très bonne heure.

Les hôtels dont les propriétaires collectionnent des coucous suisses ne sont pas vraiment propices à un sommeil profond, pas plus que ceux situés en bord de mer. Le doux lapement des vagues sur la grève est certes soporifique, mais là où l'océan fouette les rochers dans un rugissement tonitruant, vous risquez de vous

SLEEP

SCHLAFEN

There are some hotel rooms that charm with their view or decor, some that linger in memory for their location or atmosphere. But special and few are those that deliver the pleasure of a deep, satisfying sleep.

The hotels where I have slept very well all have one thing in common: beautiful white all-cotton sheets. Often, they are starched and ironed; sometimes they have the name of the hotel lovingly embroidered across the top hem. In many cases, the sheets are old, but the areas of wear have been painstakingly mended, by hand, in a web of tiny white stitches.

Deep sleep, I am convinced, is severely compromised by polyester blends.

Once the right bedding is secured, a hotel room may encourage complete relaxation in various ways. If the hotel is in a city, a double, preferably triple-glazed window is necessary to cut street noise down to a murmur. If you are in a countryside area, it's important to be in a location where roosters are prohibited. In tropical places—and even temperate ones—a billowy mosquito net (always check for holes before retiring and carry an extra few Band-Aids to plug them) and a gently spinning ceiling fan are sleep's best friends. If you are in the Middle East or India, choose the hotel that's furthest away from the local mosque, unless you want a very early wake up call.

Good sleep is hard to come by in hotels where the owners are collectors of cuckoo clocks, and not always a sure bet in seaside hotels, either. The gentle lapping of waves is soporific, but in hotels where the ocean crashes over the rocks with a great roar, you may wake up dreaming that you've gone down with the Titanic.

At hotels like the Somatheeram Ayurvedic Beach Resort, where massage and health treatments are part of the guest's daily program, satisfying sleep is almost

Manche Hotels bezaubern mit ihrer Aussicht oder ihrer Ausstattung, andere bleiben dank ihrer Lage oder Atmosphäre in Erinnerung. Aber kostbar und sehr selten sind solche, die einem die Freude eines tiefen, befriedigenden Schlafs gewähren.

Die Hotels, in denen ich sehr gut geschlafen habe, hatten alle eines gemein: wunderbar weiße Bettlaken aus reiner Baumwolle. Oft sind sie gestärkt und gebügelt, manchmal ist der Name des Hotels liebevoll am oberen Saum eingestickt. Häufig sind diese Laken schon alt, die abgenutzten Stellen aber gewissenhaft ausgebessert, von Hand, mit einem feinen Geflecht winziger, weißer Stiche.

In Polyesterbeimischungen ist ein gesunder, tiefer Schlaf kaum möglich, davon bin ich überzeugt.

Ist die richtige Bettwäsche vorhanden, kann ein Hotelzimmer die absolute Entspannung auf verschiedenste Art und Weise fördern. Liegt das Hotel in der City, sind doppelt, am liebsten dreifach verglaste Fenster von Nöten, um den Straßenlärm auf ein sanftes Rauschen zu reduzieren. Hält man sich in einer ländlichen Gegend auf, kommt es darauf an, einen Ort zu wählen, an dem Hähne verboten sind. In tropischen Gefilden – selbst in gemäßigten – sind ein Moskitonetz (man sollte es stets vor dem Schlafengehen auf Löcher überprüfen und immer ein paar Streifen Leukoplast vorrätig haben, um sie zu flicken) und ein sich leise drehender Deckenventilator die besten Gefährten des Schlafes. Bereist man den Nahen Osten oder Indien, wähle man stets das Hotel, das am weitesten von der örtlichen Moschee entfernt liegt, es sei denn, man möchte besonders früh geweckt werden.

Guten Schlaf findet man schwerlich in Hotels, deren Betreiber Kuckucksuhren sammeln, und auch nicht immer in Hotels an der Küste. Das sanfte Klatschen der

réveiller en sursaut après avoir rêvé que vous vous trouviez à bord du Titanic.

Dans des hôtels comme le Somatheeram Ayurvedic Beach Resort, où les massages et les soins corporels sont au programme de la journée, un sommeil satisfaisant est quasiment garanti. Il en va de même dans les monastères qui ouvrent leurs portes aux voyageurs. Au Shojoshin-in, un des 14 monastères zen de Koyasan, au Japon, qui offrent un refuge au gens de passage et aux pèlerins, je me suis doucement laissée emporter par les songes, bercée par les roulements lointains et profonds du gong d'un temple ancien. Ce n'était pas tout à fait le Nirvana, mais presque.

guaranteed. Likewise at monasteries that open their doors to travelers. In the Shojoshin-in, one of fourteen Zen monasteries in Koyasan, Japan, which provide lodging to guests and pilgrims, I fell gently into dreams as a sonorous, ancient temple gong tolled in the distance —perhaps not Nirvana, but close enough for me.

Wellen ist einschläfernd, aber in Hotels, vor denen sich der Ozean mit ohrenbetäubendem Tosen an den Felsen bricht, wacht man möglicherweise auf und glaubt, mit der Titanic untergegangen zu sein.

In Hotels wie dem Somatheeram Ayurvedic Beach Resort, in denen Massagen und Gesundheitsanwendungen zum Tagesprogramm des Gastes zählen, ist ein erholsamer Schlaf meistens garantiert. Gleichermaßen in Klöstern, die Reisenden ihre Pforten öffnen. Im Shojoshin-in, einem von 14 Zen-Klöstern in Koyasan in Japan, die Gästen und Pilgern Unterkunft gewähren, glitt ich sanft ins Träumen, während ein sonorer, uralter Tempelgong in der Ferne erklang – das war vielleicht noch nicht das Nirvana, aber für mich nahe genug dran.

PEACE AND PLENTY INN
AUCKLAND, NEW ZEALAND

HOTEL KÜNSTLERHEIM LUISE
BERLIN, GERMANY

LES COUPS DE FOUDRE

Je roule sur la route qui longe le lac Supérieur au nord
du Minnesota, à quelques kilomètres de la frontière ca-
nadienne, revenant vers mon hôtel. Je suis raisonnable-
ment satisfaite de la chambre que j'avais réservée au
téléphone sans avoir vu l'hôtel au préalable, mais déçue
par ce dernier. C'est un bâtiment récent préfabriqué,
style pavillon de banlieue, avec des plafonds bas et de
petites fenêtres au lieu du vieux pavillon de chasse
auquel j'avais rêvé, avec poutres apparentes, grande
cheminée et têtes de cerf empaillées au mur.

    Puis, du coin de l'œil, j'aperçois un paysage si dé-
licieux que, sans réfléchir, je décide sur-le-champ d'aller
y voir de plus près. J'arrête la voiture sur une allée en
graviers, sors et fais quelques pas sous de hauts pins
vert sombre, m'avançant vers un groupe de jolis cottages en bois blancs et bleus. Je reste là une minute,
consumée par le regret de ne pas passer la nuit au Trailside Cabins.

    Cela m'arrive parfois. En voyageant, je tombe sur
un hôtel ou une chambre d'hôtes qui me laisse sans
voix, comme un bel inconnu à l'autre bout de la pièce.
Je ne peux pas prévoir ce qui me séduira, parfois c'est
une façade couverte d'ornements magnifiques «fin de
siècle», parfois c'est la promesse d'une aventure,
comme le bungalow perché sur pilotis au-dessus de
l'Amazone.

    Ce coup de foudre pour un hôtel se produit toujours
lorsque je me suis déjà installée ailleurs et n'ai pas le
courage de déménager (ou ne peux pas parce que j'ai
payé d'avance). Je reste là à contempler le bâtiment
en soupirant. Parfois, j'entre et demande à visiter une
chambre, espérant qu'elle sera affreuse, ou trop chère,
afin d'avoir moins de regrets. De temps en temps, la
ravissante façade derrière la petite clôture en bois blanc
cache une salle de bains laide et douteuse, ainsi qu'un
matelas défoncé. Mais souvent, l'intérieur de l'hôtel est

AT FIRST SIGHT

I am driving on a narrow highway along Lake Superior in northern Minnesota, just a few miles from the Canadian border, on my way back to the hotel. I am reasonably satisfied with the room that I've booked, sight unseen, over the phone, but disappointed that the place is a newly-constructed suburban-style prefab building with low ceilings and small windows, instead of an old hunting lodge with beamed ceilings, a big fireplace, and deer heads on the wall.

Then, just out of the corner of my eye, I spot something so delightful that without thinking I pull off the highway immediately. I stop the car on the gravel driveway, get out and walk a few steps among beautiful tall dark green pine trees to a cluster of pretty white and blue clapboard cottages. I stand there a minute, consumed with regret that I'm not staying at the Trailside Cabins.

It happens sometimes, while traveling, that I will stumble across a hotel or guest house that knocks me out at first sight, like an attractive stranger across a room. There's no telling what will get to me; sometimes I fall for a facade dripping with gorgeous, fin de siecle ornamentation, other times I'm taken in by the promise of adventure, the bungalow perched on poles in the Amazon River.

Hotel Infatuation nearly always occurs when I have already established myself at another place, and don't want the hassle of moving (or can't leave, because I've paid in advance). I stare at the hotel, I sigh, and occasionally go in and ask to see a room, hoping that it will be awful, or over-priced so I will feel better about my own hotel. Sometimes I will find an ugly, dingy bathroom and saggy mattress behind the cute façade with the white picket fence. But often, the inside of the hotel is even more pleasant than its exterior. In which case I will either break down, cut my losses and check in, or torture myself over the decision until it's too late to make the move.

AUF DEN ERSTEN BLICK

Auf dem Rückweg zu meinem Hotel fahre ich eine schmale Landstraße am Lake Superior im Norden Minnesotas entlang, nur ein paar Meilen von der kanadischen Grenze entfernt. Ich bin durchaus zufrieden mit dem Zimmer, das ich unbesehen telefonisch gebucht habe, aber ein wenig enttäuscht, dass mein Hotel ein Neubau ist, ein spießiges Einfamilien-Fertighaus mit niedrigen Decken und schmalen Fenstern, und keine alte Jagdhütte mit Balkendecke, großem Kamin und ausgestopften Hirschköpfen an der Wand.

Dann entdecke ich aus dem Augenwinkel etwas so Wunderbares, dass ich sofort von der Landstraße abbiege. Ich parke den Wagen auf einem Schotterweg, steige aus und schlendere ein kleines Stück zwischen herrlichen großen, dunkelgrünen Kiefern auf eine Gruppe weiß und blau gestrichener, mit Holzschindeln gedeckter Cottages zu. Ich verharre dort einen Augenblick in tiefem Bedauern, nicht in den Trailside Cabins abgestiegen zu sein.

Manchmal widerfährt es mir, dass ich zufällig auf ein Hotel stoße, das mich beim ersten Anblick umwirft, wie ein attraktiver Fremder, der den Raum betritt. Es ist nicht vorauszusagen, was mich beeindruckt; manchmal fasziniert mich eine mit Fin-de-Siècle-Ornamenten überladene Fassade, manchmal begeistert mich die Aussicht auf ein Abenteuer, wie bei dem Bungalow, der auf Pfählen über dem Amazonas thronte.

Dass ich mich Hals über Kopf in ein Hotel verliebe, passiert mir meistens dann, wenn ich mich schon woanders eingemietet habe und mir nicht die Mühe machen will, umzuziehen, oder nicht raus kann, weil ich im Voraus bezahlt habe. Ich starre das Hotel an, seufze, und manchmal gehe ich auch hinein und lasse mir ein Zimmer zeigen, in der Hoffnung, es scheußlich oder überteuert zu finden, damit mir bei meinem eigenen Hotelzimmer wohler ist. Manchmal finde ich dann ein

encore plus charmant que l'extérieur. Auquel cas, soit je craque, casse ma tirelire et prends une chambre, soit je tergiverse jusqu'à ce qu'il soit trop tard pour faire le transfert.

Naturellement, les façades peuvent aussi avoir sur moi l'effet inverse. J'arrive quelque part et veux prendre mes jambes à mon cou avant même d'avoir pénétré dans la réception. J'ai ainsi failli m'enfuir du Green Yard Hotel, en Corée, parce qu'il ressemblait trop à une galerie commerçante équipée d'une patinoire. Mais il n'y avait nulle part où aller. Heureusement, j'avais réservé l'une des chambres les moins chères de l'hôtel. Celles-ci se trouvaient dans une annexe d'un étage, cachée parmi les sapins qui me masquaient la vue sur le verre et le béton.

Une autre fois, j'étais en train de m'éclipser en douce d'un petit hôtel peu engageant situé dans une rue bondée au centre de Séoul. J'étais déjà dehors quand une vieille dame s'est précipitée derrière moi, m'a attrapé le poignet de sa petite main noueuse et m'a traînée malgré moi de nouveau à l'intérieur puis dans l'escalier. La chambre contenait un lit double, une salle de bains et une télévision. Elle était propre et sentait le linge frais.

Que pouvais-je faire? J'ai souri et acquiescé, acceptant mon sort comme on accepte un mariage arrangé. Elle a enfin relâché sa poigne de fer. Peut-être qu'avec le temps, je finirais par tomber amoureuse de son hôtel.

Of course, exteriors sometimes have the opposite effect on me. I'll arrive somewhere, and want to flee before I've even entered the lobby. I almost ran away from the Green Yard Hotel, in Korea, because it looked too much like a shopping mall with an ice skating rink. But there was nowhere to run; the Green Yard is in the middle of a Korean national park, miles from nowhere. Luckily for me, I'd booked one of the hotel's cheapest rooms, located in a two-story annex hidden among tall fir trees that blocked the view of glass and concrete.

Once I was in the midst of running away from an unpromising-looking guesthouse located in a densely crowded lane in downtown Seoul. As I was turning to go back down the alley, an elderly woman ran out of the doorway, grabbed my wrist with her small bony hand, and physically pulled me into the building and up the stairs. The room contained a double bed, a bathroom and a television. It was clean, and smelled like fresh laundry.

What could I do? I smiled and nodded, accepting my fate like an arranged marriage. She released me from her knotty grip. Maybe I would fall in love with her hotel, over time.

hässliches, schmuddeliges Badezimmer und eine durchgelegene Matratze hinter der hübschen Fassade mit dem weißen Palisadenzaun. Aber oft ist das Innere eines solchen Hotels sogar noch ansprechender als das Äußere. Entweder kapituliere ich dann, schreibe meine Verluste ab und checke ein, oder ich quäle mich solange mit einer Entscheidung herum, bis es zu spät ist, umzuziehen.

Natürlich hat die äußere Erscheinung manchmal die gegenteilige Wirkung auf mich. Ich komme irgendwo an und möchte schon Reißaus nehmen, bevor ich die Lobby betreten habe. Ich wäre beinahe vor dem Green Yard Hotel in Korea davongelaufen, weil es mich fatal an ein Einkaufszentrum mit Eislaufbahn erinnerte. Aber es gab nichts, wohin ich hätte fliehen können, denn das Green Yard liegt in einem koreanischen Nationalpark, mitten im Nirgendwo. Glücklicherweise hatte ich eines der billigsten Zimmer gebucht, und das lag in einem zweistöckigen Nebengebäude, versteckt zwischen hohen Tannen, die den Blick auf Glas und Beton verstellten.

Einmal war ich drauf und dran, vor einer wenig vielversprechend aussehenden Pension in einer dicht bevölkerten Gasse im Zentrum Seouls die Flucht zu ergreifen. Als ich mich abwandte und weggehen wollte, stürzte eine ältere Frau aus dem Eingang, packte mich mit ihrer kleinen, knochigen Hand am Handgelenk und zerrte mich gewaltsam ins Gebäude und die Treppen hoch. Das Zimmer verfügte über ein Doppelbett, ein Badezimmer und einen Fernseher. Es war sauber und roch nach frischer Wäsche.

Was blieb mir da anderes übrig? Ich lächelte und nickte, ich akzeptierte mein Schicksal wie eine Vernunftehe. Sie entließ mich aus ihrem knorrigen Griff. Vielleicht würde ich mit der Zeit ja lernen, ihr Hotel zu lieben …

Cela m'arrive parfois. En voyageant, je tombe sur un hôtel ou une chambre
d'hôtes qui me laisse sans voix, comme un bel inconnu à l'autre bout de
la pièce.

Sometimes, while traveling, I will stumble across a hotel or guest house
that knocks me out at first sight, like an attractive stranger across a room.

Manchmal widerfährt es mir während einer Reise, dass ich zufällig auf ein
Hotel stoße, das mich bereits beim ersten Anblick umwirft, wie ein attraktiver Fremder, der den Raum betritt.

DIX ENDROITS OÙ J'AI ÉTÉ TRÈS HEUREUSE

TEN PLACES I WAS HAPPY

ZEHN HOTELS, IN DENEN ICH MICH
SEHR WOHL FÜHLTE

UN ONE EINS

Casa La Punta, La Gomera, îles Canaries: parce que je pouvais m'asseoir sur le balcon et admirer le volcan.

Casa La Punta, La Gomera, Canary Islands: Because I could sit on the balcony and admire the volcano.

Casa La Punta, La Gomera, Kanarische Inseln: Weil ich auf dem Balkon sitzen und den Vulkan bewundern konnte.

DEUX TWO ZWEI

Somatheeram Ayurvedic Beach Resort, Kerala, Inde: parce que, tous les jours, quatre femmes venaient déverser de l'huile chaude sur mon corps.

Somatheeram Ayurvedic Beach Resort, Kerala, India: Because every day four women came and poured warm oil all over my body.

Somatheeram Ayurvedic Beach Resort, Kerala, Indien: Weil dort jeden Tag vier Frauen warmes Öl über meinen ganzen Körper träufelten.

TROIS THREE DREI

Les Good Karma Bungalows, Bali: parce que juste devant ma porte s'étendait un océan rempli de poissons-perroquets.

The Good Karma Bungalows, Bali: Because at my doorstep was an ocean filled with parrot fish.

Die Good Karma Bungalows, Bali: Weil vor meiner Schwelle ein Ozean voller Papageienfische lag.

QUATRE FOUR VIER

A bord du SS Nadson Jeane, sur le fleuve Amazone, Brésil: parce que chaque fois que l'embarcation tanguait, 100 hamacs se balançaient à l'unisson.

Onboard the SS Nadson Jeane, on the Amazon, Brazil: Because when the ship rocked, 100 hammocks swung in unison.

An Bord der SS Nadson Jeane auf dem Amazonas, Brasilien: Weil jedes Mal 100 Hängematten im Gleichklang schaukelten, wenn das Schiff von den Wellen bewegt wurde.

CINQ FIVE FÜNF

Hotel Europa, Florence, Italie: parce que je pouvais ouvrir ma fenêtre et voir le Duomo.

Hotel Europa, Florence, Italy: Because I could open my window and see the Duomo.

Hotel Europa, Florenz, Italien: Weil ich mein Fenster öffnen und den Dom sehen konnte.

SIX SIX SECHS

Lani 1 Guest House, Vientiane, Laos: parce que des moines habitaient juste à côté.

Lani 1 Guest House, Vientiane, Laos: Because monks lived next door.

Lani 1 Guest House, Vientiane, Laos: Weil gleich nebenan Mönche lebten.

SEPT SEVEN SIEBEN

Casa de la Playa, Siquijor, Philippines: parce que la plage était rose et déserte et que les chiens étaient gentils.

Casa de la Playa, Siquijor, Philippines: Because the beach was pink and empty, and the dogs were friendly.

Casa de la Playa, Siquijor, Philippinen: Weil der Strand makellos und leer und die Hunde freundlich waren.

HUIT EIGHT ACHT

La Veranda, Bocas del Toro, Panama: parce qu'une pluie tropicale crépitait doucement sur le toit en tôle ondulée.

La Veranda, Bocas del Toro, Panama: Because a tropical rain hammered gently on the corrugated iron roof.

La Veranda, Bocas del Toro, Panama: Weil ein tropischer Regen sanft auf das Wellblechdach prasselte.

NEUF NINE NEUN

Broadlands Lodging House, Madras, Inde: parce qu'il y avait les éléphants.

Broadlands Lodging House, Madras, India: Because of the elephants.

Broadlands Lodging House, Madras, Indien: wegen der Elefanten.

DIX TEN ZEHN

Candidasa Gandhi Ashram, Bali: parce que nous récitions des incantations au crépuscule entourés de bougies et de fleurs d'hibiscus.

Candidasa Gandhi Ashram, Bali: Because we chanted at dusk over candles and hibiscus flowers.

Candidasa Ghandi Ashram, Bali: Weil wir bei Einbruch der Dunkelheit bei Kerzenlicht und Hibiskusblüten gemeinsam sangen.

LES MOINS CHERS DES HÔTELS
LES MOINS CHERS

La voyageuse d'Amsterdam secoue la tête d'un air aba-
sourdi et je n'arrive pas à décider si c'est par pitié ou
parce qu'elle me croit sotte. Je me replonge donc dans
mon thé à la menthe. Il m'avait pourtant semblé que 20
dollars la nuit pour ma chambre single au Cosmopolitan
Hotel du Caire était une excellente affaire. Toutefois, au
cours de mes voyages, j'ai appris une chose: vous avez
beau penser que votre hôtel est bon marché, vous trou-
verez toujours un autre voyageur qui vous affirmera,
avec un sourire triomphant ou un soupir compatissant,
qu'on vous gruge.

   Au début, je le prenais à cœur, jusqu'à ce que je me
rende compte que l'obsession d'épargner 5 ou 10 dollars
était un art de la surenchère pratiqué entre adeptes des
voyages pas chers. J'ai fini par comprendre que, comme
dans le cas de nombreux autres produits mondiaux, il
y a rarement un lien direct entre les prix pratiqués par
un hôtel et la valeur réelle de la chambre. Le prix d'une
chambre sur le marché fluctue comme les titres boursiers
et dépend de nombreux facteurs: l'économie locale,
nationale, mondiale; la popularité du site; si votre visite
coïncide ou non avec le congrès annuel de la Confrérie
Internationale des Ajusteurs de Hottes de Cuisine.

   Parfois, lorsque je prépare un voyage, je me sens
un peu comme un charognard, parcourant la presse
internationale en quête d'informations qui pourraient me
conduire dans un lieu de vacances merveilleux et bon
marché. Dans l'idéal, je recherche un pays dont le gouvernement a été récemment (mais pas trop récemment)
renversé lors d'un coup d'état rapide et indolore, dont la
devise a été brusquement et radicalement dévaluée, ou
qui a été traversé depuis peu par une tempête tropicale
qui a fait les gros titres dans les médias mais peu de
dégâts. Lorsque j'ai enfin découvert cet endroit, je me
glisse sur la pointe des pieds dans l'accalmie entre la
calamité et le retour des charters.

You are paying twenty dollars a night for your
room? That is far too much!"

„Sie zahlen 20 Dollar pro Nacht für Ihr Zimmer?
Das ist viel zuviel!"

THE CHEAPEST CHEAP HOTELS

DAS PREISWERTESTE PREISWERTE HOTEL

The woman traveler from Amsterdam shakes her head
in dismay, and I can't tell whether she pities me or thinks
I am a fool. So I go back to sipping my mint tea. It had
seemed to me that the $20 I was paying for my single
room in the Cosmopolitan Hotel in Cairo was a phenom-
enally good deal. However, one of the things I've learned
while traveling a lot is this: No matter how cheap you
think your hotel is, you will always meet some fellow
traveler who will tell you, either with a triumphant smirk
or a pitying sigh, that you're being overcharged.

I used to take this to heart, until I realized that mak-
ing a fetish out of saving $5 or $10 was a form of one-
upmanship among hard-core budget travelers. And, as I
stayed in more and more modestly priced hotels all over
the world, I began to understand that, as with so many
other global commodities, there is often little correlation
between a hotel room's asking price and its real value.
The market price of a hotel room fluctuates like the stock
market, and depends on many things—local, national
and global economics, the popularity of the location,
and whether or not your visit happens to coincide with
the annual convention of the International Brotherhood
of Steam Pipe Fitters.

Sometimes, planning my trips, I feel a bit like an
ambulance chaser, scouring international newspapers
for information that might lead me to a wonderful, inexpensive travel spot. Ideally, I am looking for a country
whose government has recently (but not too recently)
fallen in a swift, painless coup d' etat, or whose currency
has been suddenly and drastically devalued, or where
there has been a recent tropical storm that made big
headlines, but caused little serious damage. When I find
this place, I tiptoe gently into that lull between calamity
and the return of chartered tour groups.

While I try not to obsess about nickels and dimes
when it comes to hotel rooms, I have come to realize

Die Urlauberin aus Amsterdam schüttelt bestürzt den
Kopf, und ich weiß nicht, ob sie mich bedauert oder für
dumm hält. Also widme ich mich wieder meinem Pfeffer-
minztee. Mir waren die 20 Dollar, die ich für mein Einzel-
zimmer im Cosmopolitan Hotel in Kairo zahlte, als sensa-
tionell gutes Geschäft erschienen. Eines habe ich jedoch
während meines intensiven Reisens gelernt: Ganz gleich,
wie preiswert man sein Hotel findet, man trifft immer einen
anderen Reisenden, der einem mit triumphierendem Grin-
sen oder mitleidigem Seufzen erklärt, man sei über den
Tisch gezogen worden.

Früher nahm ich mir das zu Herzen, bis ich irgend-
wann begriff, dass eingefleischte Budget-Reisende einen
Sport daraus machen, 5 oder 10 Dollar sparen zu wollen.
Und nachdem ich in mehr und mehr Hotels mit moderaten
Preisen abgestiegen war, begann ich zu verstehen, dass
der verlangte Preis, wie bei so vielen internationalen Han-
delsgütern, oft wenig über den tatsächlichen Wert einer
Ware oder Dienstleistung aussagt. Der Marktpreis eines
Hotelzimmers ist Schwankungen unterworfen wie die Börse
und von vielen Faktoren abhängig – von der lokalen, natio-
nalen und internationalen Wirtschaftslage, von der Beliebt-
heit des Reiseziels oder davon, ob der Besuch zufällig mit
der Jahreskonferenz der Internationalen Bruderschaft der
Heizungsrohrverleger zusammenfällt oder nicht.

Wenn ich bei der Vorbereitung meiner Trips internationale Zeitungen nach Informationen durchforste, die
mich zu einem wundervollen, preiswerten Fleckchen Erde
führen könnten, fühle ich mich manchmal wie einer dieser
Rechtsanwälte, die noch am Unfallort Opfer als Klienten
zu gewinnen versuchen. Im Idealfall finde ich ein Land,
dessen Regierung erst kürzlich (aber nicht zu kürzlich)
einem raschen, einigermaßen unblutigen Staatsstreich
zum Opfer gefallen ist, dessen Währung plötzlich dras-
tisch abgewertet wurde oder das gerade von einem Tro-
pensturm heimgesucht wurde, der zwar große Schlag-

Good Karma Beach
BUNGALOWS
Dusun Selang Amed, Amlapura
B a l i

120 No. .005061

Number	Date	Meals	Price
	le juin	Room 2 night	9 USA 252'000
	out	Food & Drink	84000
		Transport to airport.	160'000
		Total R,p.	496'000

Guest Signature,   Waiter Signature,

(...............................)   (...............................)

We wish you would like to enjoy our food

Si j'essaie de ne pas faire une fixation sur les petites économies, je me suis rendue compte que les chambres les moins chères de ces chambres pas chères, celles qui ne m'ont pas coûté plus de 25 dollars la nuit, sont celles dont je me souviens le mieux et avec le plus d'attendrissement. Chacune avait un détail qui la sortait de l'ordinaire, de jolis draps fleuris aux couleurs vives et des murs tapissés de tapa polynésien à Fifita Guest House à Tonga, une étrange cloison en fer forgé Art Déco dans la salle de bains de la Peachy Guest House à Bangkok. Ces hôtels ont aussi souvent des propriétaires exubérants et accueillants comme M. Keo Sithan, du Golden Apsara à Siem Reap, au Cambodge, qui, en me servant le café un matin m'a raconté l'histoire émouvante de sa fuite devant les Khmers rouges. Après avoir passé la nuit chez Doña Maria, dans le village espagnol de Camelle, elle m'a préparé le petit déjeuner et a glissé un sandwich au chorizo dans mon sac à dos pendant que je regardais ailleurs.

Au moment de quitter les Good Karma Bungalows à Bali, Baba, le propriétaire, m'a tendu sa carte de visite imprimée à la main. Elle ne disait pas: «Venez dans mon hôtel pour ses belles petites chaumières traditionnelles sur une plage tranquille de la côte est de Bali, ses vues magnifiques, ses couchers de soleil spectaculaires et son excellente plongée sous-marine». Elle disait simplement: «Venez bavarder et rire de bon karma avec Baba».

Bavarder, rire, de jolis draps, des sandwichs au chorizo – le bon karma d'un hôtel se sent tout de suite, il est difficile à définir et il est impossible de mettre un prix dessus.

that the cheapest of these cheap rooms—the ones that I spent $25 or less to stay in—happen to be the rooms that I remember most clearly, and most fondly. Each had some detail that lifted it above the ordinary—pretty sheets with bright flowers and walls covered with Polynesian tapa cloth at Fifita Guest House in Tonga, curious Art Deco iron grillwork in the bathroom of Peachy Guest House in Bangkok. Often, they also had exuberant, welcoming owners like Mr. Keo Sithan, of the Golden Apsara in Siem Reap, Cambodia, who served me coffee one morning and told me the moving story of his escape from the Khmer Rouge. When I stayed the night at Doña Maria's house, in the Spanish village of Camelle, she cooked me breakfast and tucked a chorizo sandwich into my backpack when I wasn't looking.

As I was leaving the Good Karma Bungalows in Bali, Baba, the owner, handed me his hand-printed card. It did not say, "Come to my hotel for its collection of beautifully realized traditional thatched cottages on a remote beach in eastern Bali, for fantastic views, spectacular sunsets, and excellent snorkeling." It said, simply, "Come for talking and joking good karma with Baba."

Talking and joking, pretty sheets, chorizo sandwiches—a hotel's good karma is easy to feel, hard to pin down, and impossible to put a price on.

zeilen gemacht, aber nur wenige ernsthafte Schäden angerichtet hat. Wenn ich einen solchen Ort entdecke, genieße ich klammheimlich die Ruhe nach dem Sturm und vor der Rückkehr der Pauschalreisenden.

Während ich versuche, nicht zu sehr auf den Cent zu achten, wenn es um Hotelzimmer geht, bin ich zu der Einsicht gelangt, dass die preiswertesten dieser preiswerten Zimmer – diejenigen, für die ich 25 Dollar oder weniger bezahlt habe – auch die Zimmer sind, an die ich mich am deutlichsten und liebsten erinnere. In jedem von ihnen gab es ein kleines Detail, das es von den übrigen unterschied – hübsche Laken mit heiterem Blumenmuster und mit polynesischen Bastmatten bespannte Wände im Fifita Guest House in Tonga, das kuriose schmiedeeiserne Art-déco-Gitterfenster im Badezimmer des Peachy Guest House in Bangkok. Oft empfangen die Besitzer ihre Gäste überschwänglich und herzlich, wie Mr. Keo Sithan vom Golden Apsara in Siem Reap, Kambodscha, der mir eines Morgens Kaffee servierte und mir die bewegende Geschichte seiner Flucht vor den Roten Khmer erzählte. Als ich in Doña Marias Haus in dem spanischen Dorf Camelle übernachtete, bereitete sie mir das Frühstück und packte mir, als ich gerade nicht hinsah, ein Chorizo-Sandwich in meinen Rucksack.

Als ich die Good Karma Bungalows in Bali verließ, reichte mir Baba, der Besitzer, sein handkopiertes Kärtchen. Darauf stand nicht: „Besuchen Sie mein Hotel mit entzückend gebauten, traditionellen strohgedeckten Cottages an einem abgelegenen Strand in Ost-Bali und genießen Sie fantastische Ausblicke, spektakuläre Sonnenuntergände und exzellente Tauchgründe." Sie sagte schlicht: „Kommen Sie zum Reden und Lachen für gutes Karma mit Baba."

Reden, Lachen, hübsche Laken, Chorizo-Sandwiches – das gute Karma eines Hotels ist sofort spürbar, schwer zu beschreiben und unmöglich in Geld umzurechnen.

Si j'essaie de ne pas faire une fixation sur les petites économies, je me suis rendue compte que les chambres les moins chères de ces chambres pas chères, celles qui ne m'ont pas coûté plus de 25 dollars la nuit, sont celles dont je me souviens le mieux et avec le plus d'attendrissement.

While I try not to obsess about nickels and dimes when it comes to hotel rooms, I have come to realize that the cheapest of these cheap rooms—the ones that I spent $25 or less to stay in—happen to be the rooms that I remember most clearly, and most fondly.

Während ich versuche, nicht zu sehr auf den Cent zu achten, wenn es um Hotelzimmer geht, bin ich zu der Einsicht gelangt, dass die preiswertesten dieser preiswerten Zimmer – diejenigen, für die ich 25 Dollar oder weniger bezahlt habe – auch die Zimmer sind, an die ich mich am deutlichsten und liebsten erinnere.

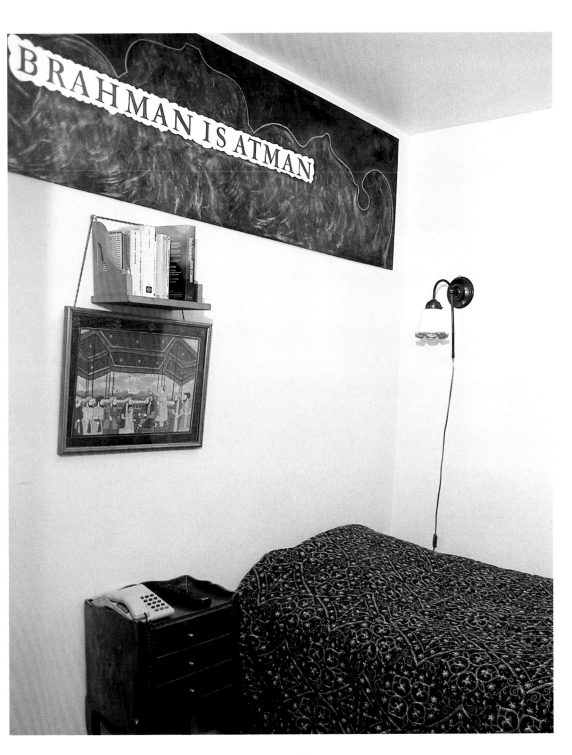

L'ESPACE

Dans de nombreuses villes, moins vous payez pour votre chambre d'hôtel, plus vous risquez de dormir dans une pièce où vous pouvez toucher simultanément deux murs se faisant face.

Jusqu'à quel degré de miniaturisation êtes-vous prêt à aller? Cela dépend de chacun. Prenez deux mesures: A) Jusqu'où s'avancent vos pieds hors du matelas? B) Quand vous êtes assis dans votre lit, combien de centimètres reste-t-il entre le sommet de votre crâne et le plafond? Soustrayez A de B, convertissez les centimètres en pouces ou inversement, multipliez le résultat par le nombre de nuits que vous avez réservé, divisez ce chiffre par le prix de la chambre – et n'oubliez pas d'emporter votre calculette.

En fait, j'aime assez les petites chambres, notamment dans des pays comme le Japon, où tout le monde vit dans de petits espaces. Il existe des dizaines de détails et d'avantages qui rendent la vie en miniature plus confortable. J'aime pouvoir enrouler mon lit et le ranger dans un placard. Et je suis très contente de ma petite lampe à col de cygne que je peux approcher du lit en la faisant glisser sur le parquet pour lire et que je peux repousser dans un coin quand je veux dormir. Une télévision avec un écran de 22 cm ou pas de télévision du tout, cela m'est égal. Une penderie? Un bureau? Je n'en ai pas besoin maintenant que j'ai découvert que ma garde-robe de voyage peut se convertir en tentures murales décoratives.

Vous vous souvenez de l'histoire du philosophe grec Diogène? Parti parcourir le monde en quête d'un homme honnête, il n'emporta avec lui qu'un tonneau, une écuelle de fer blanc et une lanterne. Un jour, apercevant un petit garçon qui buvait de l'eau dans ses mains en coupe, il se rendit compte que son écuelle était superflue et la jeta. Ce précurseur du logement minimaliste dormait et se baignait dans son tonneau.

146

SPACE

PLATZ

In many cities, the less money you are able to pay for a hotel room, the more likely it is that you will end up sleeping in a place where you can touch two opposite walls at once.

How small a living space can you handle? This is a personal matter, but I've found the following formula helpful. Take two measurements: (A) How far do your feet hang over the edge of the mattress? (B) When you sit up in bed, how many inches of space remain between the top of your head and the ceiling? Subtract A from B, convert inches to centimeters or vice versa, multiply the result by the number of nights you've reserved, divide this figure by the price of the room—and don't forget to bring your calculator.

Actually, I often enjoy staying in small rooms, particularly in countries like Japan, where living in small spaces is what everyone does. There are dozens of details and conveniences to make living in miniature more comfortable. I like being able to roll up my bed and put it in a closet, and I'm very happy to be assigned a little gooseneck lamp that I can move across the floor to the bedside when I want to read, then banish to a corner when I'm sleeping. A 9-inch television, or no television at all, is fine with me. Clothes closets? Bureaus? I don't need them now that I've discovered that my travel wardrobe can lead a double life as decorative wall hangings.

Remember the story of the ancient Greek philosopher, Diogenes? He was the philosopher who traveled around the world searching for an honest man, while carrying no baggage except a bathtub, a tin cup, and a lantern. One day Diogenes saw a little boy drinking water using his hands as a ladle, and he decided the tin cup was superfluous, and ditched it. This pioneer of minimalist accommodations slept in his bathtub.

I remembered this story one afternoon as I tried to come to grips with my "room with Western style bath" at

In vielen Städten gilt: Je weniger man für sein Hotel ausgeben kann, desto größer ist die Wahrscheinlichkeit, in einem Zimmer zu landen, in dem man mit ausgestreckten Armen zwei gegenüberliegende Wände berühren kann.

Wie viel Platzmangel lässt sich ertragen? Das ist bei jedem anders, aber ich habe mir immer mit einer Faustregel beholfen. Nehmen Sie zwei Maße: A) Wie weit ragen Ihre Füße über die Matratze hinaus? B) Wie viel Platz bleiben zwischen Ihrem Kopf und der Decke, wenn Sie aufrecht im Bett sitzen? Subtrahieren Sie A von B, rechnen Sie Inches in Zentimeter um oder umgekehrt, multiplizieren Sie das Ergebnis mit der Zahl der Übernachtungen, die Sie gebucht haben, teilen Sie dann das Ergebnis durch den Preis des Zimmers – und vergessen Sie nicht, Ihren Taschenrechner mitzunehmen.

Tatsächlich hat es mir oft Spaß gemacht, in kleinen Zimmern zu übernachten, besonders in Ländern wie Japan, wo jedermann auf kleinem Raum lebt. Es gibt Dutzende von Details und Annehmlichkeiten, die das Leben in Miniaturausgabe komfortabler machen. Ich mag es, wenn ich mein Bett zusammenrollen und in einen Schrank packen kann, ich bin sehr angetan, wenn ich eine kleine Schwanenhalslampe bekomme, die ich neben das Bett ziehen kann, wenn ich lesen, und in die Ecke verbannen, wenn ich schlafen will. Ein Mini-Fernseher oder gar kein Fernseher ist mir nur recht. Kleiderschränke? Kommoden? Die brauche ich nicht, nachdem ich herausgefunden habe, dass meine Reisegarderobe ein Doppelleben als dekorativer Wandbehang führen kann.

Ich erinnere an die Geschichte des griechischen Philosophen Diogenes. Das war der Philosoph, der auf der Suche nach einem anständigen Menschen die Welt bereiste und als Gepäck lediglich eine Tonne, eine Blechtasse und eine Lampe mit sich führte. Eines Tages sah

Cette histoire me revint en mémoire un après-midi alors que je me débattais avec ma «chambre équipée d'une salle de bains à l'occidentale» au Ryokan Shigetsu à Tokyo. La salle de bain minuscule n'avait pas de baignoire, ni même de compartiment de douche, juste un lavabo et un w.-c. coincés dans un espace si petit que je devais m'asseoir de biais sur la cuvette pour pouvoir fermer la porte. Au moment où je décidai de descendre à la réception pour me plaindre, j'aperçus le pommeau de douche: suspendu à un tuyau près du lavabo. Un astucieux architecte d'intérieur japonais avait fusionné les fonctions de douche, de lavabo, de w.-c. et de bidet en un tout unifié, l'essence même de la salle de bain.

Diogène aurait sûrement apprécié.

Ryokan Shigetsu in Tokyo. The miniscule bathroom had no bathtub. There was no shower stall, either, only a sink and a toilet crammed in so closely together that I had to sit on the toilet sideways to get the door closed. Just as I was about to go down to the reception and complain, I spotted the shower—it was hanging from a hose beside the sink. The clever, space-saving Japanese designer had collapsed the functions of shower, sink, toilet and bidet into a unified whole, the essence of bathroom.

Diogenes, I am sure, would have been very happy here.

Diogenes einen kleinen Jungen, der beim Wassertrinken seine Hände als Schöpfkelle benutzte, beschloss darauf, dass seine Tasse überflüssig war und warf sie fort. Dieser Pionier minimalistischer Unterbringung schlief in seiner Tonne.

An diese Geschichte musste ich eines Nachmittags denken, als ich versuchte, mit meinem „Zimmer mit westlichem Bad" im Ryokan Shigetsu in Tokio zurechtzukommen. Das winzige Bad hatte keine Wanne. Eine Dusche gab es auch nicht, nur ein Waschbecken und eine Toilette, so eng zusammen hineingezwängt, dass ich seitlich auf der Toilette sitzen musste, um die Tür schließen zu können. Gerade als ich zur Rezeption gehen und mich beschweren wollte, entdeckte ich die Dusche – sie hing an einem Schlauch neben dem Waschbecken. Der clevere, Platz sparende japanische Designer hatte die Funktionen von Dusche, Waschbecken, Toilette und Bidet zu einem Ganzen zusammengefasst, zur Essenz eines Badezimmers.

Ich bin sicher, Diogenes hätte sich dort sehr wohl gefühlt.

Dans de nombreuses villes, moins vous payez pour votre chambre d'hôtel, plus vous risquez de dormir dans une pièce où vous pouvez toucher simultanément deux murs se faisant face.

In many cities, the less money you are able to pay for a hotel room, the more likely it is that you will end up sleeping in a place where you can touch two opposite walls at once.

In vielen Städten gilt: Je weniger man für sein Hotel ausgeben kann, desto größer ist die Wahrscheinlichkeit, in einem Zimmer zu landen, in dem man mit ausgestreckten Armen zwei gegenüberliegende Wände berühren kann.

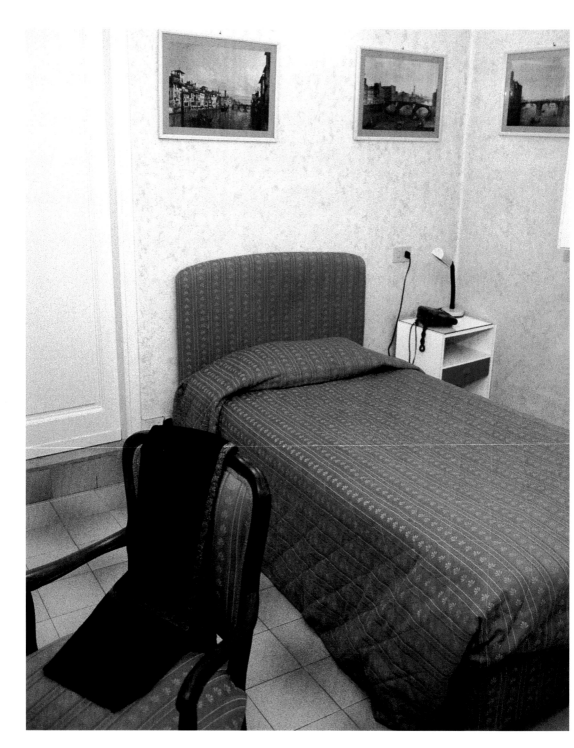

LA VUE

Même les plus agréables des chambres d'hôtels ont entre leurs murs un petit quelque chose de mélancolique. Lorsque vous débarquez quelque part, la chambre est votre nouvelle amie, vous ne voyez qu'elle. Vous ouvrez tous les tiroirs, essayez tous les interrupteurs, jouez avec les robinets, entamez une nouvelle relation. Mais la chambre ne sera jamais aussi excitante et importante à vos yeux qu'au cours de ces premières heures. Après tout, vous n'avez pas fait tout ce chemin rien que pour regarder ce qu'il y a dans le mini-bar. Chaque soir, la chambre perd un peu de son aura tandis que vous découvrez et explorez le monde encore plus intriguant qui l'entoure. Puis, finalement, vous remballez vos affaires, lui faites vos adieux et l'abandonnez à quelqu'un d'autre.

Ainsi soit-il.

Pour étouffer cette tristesse, j'essaye toujours de trouver une chambre qui retiendra plus longtemps mon attention, une dont le charme se fanera moins vite. Une chambre avec vue.

Cette dernière n'a pas besoin d'être un paysage de carte postale à couper le souffle, bien qu'il soit toujours exaltant d'ouvrir grand les rideaux et de se retrouver face à un port de pêche ensoleillé rempli de bateaux pastel, ou des sommets alpins enneigés se dressant au-dessus des sapins. Mais je trouve encore plus excitant d'ouvrir ma fenêtre sur une scène de la vie quotidienne: des piétons madrilènes armés de parapluie pressant le pas dans une rue pavée; ou une famille romaine vivant sur le toit voisin.

Au Caire, je suis assise sur mon petit balcon à l'hôtel al-Hussein. C'est vendredi et, en contrebas, un millier d'hommes s'agenouillent dans un même mouvement, priant à l'unisson. Un soir à Hong Kong, au Bishop Lei International House, ma vue sur le port explose soudain en un spectaculaire feu d'artifice à l'occasion d'une célébration à laquelle la ville n'est pas encore habituée: l'anni-

THE VIEW

DIE AUSSICHT

Hotel rooms, even the most pleasant ones, contain within their walls a hint of melancholy. When you arrive in a place, the room is your new friend, all-important. You open all the drawers, turn all the lights on and off, play with the faucets, and begin a new relationship. But the room is never as exciting or important to you as it is in those first few hours. You have not traveled all this way, after all, just to check out the mini-bar. Each night, the room's allure fades ever so slightly, as you discover and explore the even more intriguing world outside its limits. And then, finally, you say goodbye, pack up and leave it to someone else.

As it must be.

To quell this sadness, I always try to find a room with more staying power, one whose appeal doesn't fade so quickly. A room with a view.

It doesn't have to be a knockout picture-postcard vista, although it's exhilarating to sweep aside a curtain to pastel boats in a sunny blue harbor, or a snowy Alpine peak rising above pine trees. But I get even more of a thrill opening my window on an everyday scene: pedestrians with umbrellas scurrying down a cobbled street in Madrid, or a family living on an adjacent rooftop, in Rome.

In Cairo, I sit on my little balcony in the Hotel al-Hussein. It is Friday, and below me a thousand men are on their hands and knees, praying in unison. In Hong Kong, at the Bishop Lei International House, my view of the harbor explodes in spectacular fireworks one evening, during a celebration that's new for this city, the anniversary of China's communist revolution. The skylines of Berlin and Kuala Lumpur seem permanently under construction; the skylines of Seoul and Bangkok, chaotic, interchangeable Asian tigers.

Hotelzimmern, selbst den einladendsten, haftet ein Hauch des Melancholischen an. Wenn Sie an einem Ort eintreffen, ist das Zimmer Ihr neuer Freund, wichtiger als alles andere. Sie ziehen alle Schubladen auf, schalten das Licht an und aus, spielen mit den Wasserhähnen und knüpfen eine neue Beziehung an. Aber das Zimmer ist nie wieder so aufregend und wichtig wie während dieser ersten paar Stunden. Schließlich ist man nicht den weiten Weg gereist, um die Mini-Bar zu überprüfen. Mit jeder Nacht verblasst der Reiz des Zimmers ein klein wenig, während man die noch faszinierendere Welt außerhalb seiner Grenzen entdeckt und erforscht. Und irgendwann sagen Sie bye-bye, packen zusammen und überlassen es jemand anderem.

Das ist der Lauf der Welt.

Um diesen traurigen Moment hinauszuschieben, bin ich immer auf der Suche nach einem Zimmer, das mich länger halten kann, eines, dessen Reiz nicht so schnell verblasst. Ein Zimmer mit Aussicht.

Es muss keine umwerfende Postkartenszenerie sein, so berauschend es auch ist, den Vorhang beiseite zu ziehen und pastellfarbene Boote in einem sonnigen, azurblauen Hafen zu sehen oder einen schneebedeckten Alpengipfel, der über den Kiefernkronen aufragt. Ich finde es jedoch noch schöner, wenn ich von meinem Fenster auf eine Alltagsszene blicke: Passanten mit Regenschirmen, die eine Straße mit Kopfsteinpflaster in Madrid entlanghasten, oder eine Familie in Rom, die auf einem angrenzenden Dach lebt.

In Kairo sitze ich auf meinem kleinen Balkon im Hotel al-Hussein. Es ist Freitag, und zu meinen Füßen knien tausend einstimmig betende Männer. In Hongkong im Bishop Lei International House explodiert eines Abends im Hafen vor meinem Fenster ein spektakuläres Feuerwerk – der Anlass ist ein Fest, das für die Stadt

versaire de la révolution communiste chinoise. Les sil-
houettes de Berlin et de Kuala Lumpur ressemblent à un
chantier permanent. Chaotiques, celles de Séoul et de
Bangkok sont comme des tigres asiatiques interchan-
geables.

Une chambre avec une telle vue est plus qu'un
simple endroit où dormir et se doucher. C'est le seuil d'un
lieu et d'une culture à découvrir. Je me tiens devant ma
fenêtre, observant, m'apprêtant une fois de plus à pénétrer dans un nouveau monde.

A room with such a view is more than just a place to sleep and shower, it is a threshold to an unfamiliar place and culture. I stand at my hotel room window, watching. And prepare to enter another new world.

noch ganz neu ist, der Jahrestag der chinesischen Revolution. An den Skylines von Berlin und Kuala Lumpur scheint ständig gebaut zu werden; die Skylines von Seoul und Bangkok sind chaotische, austauschbare Bilder von asiatischen Tigerstaaten.

Ein Zimmer mit einer solchen Aussicht ist mehr als ein Raum zum Schlafen und Duschen, es ist die Schwelle zu einem unbekannten Ort. Ich stehe an meinem Hotelzimmerfenster und beobachte. Ich mache mich bereit, eine neue Welt zu betreten.

Je me tiens devant ma fenêtre, observant, m'apprêtant une fois de plus
à pénétrer dans un nouveau monde.

I stand at my hotel room window, watching. And prepare to enter
another new world.

Ich stehe an meinem Hotelzimmerfenster und beobachte. Ich mache
mich bereit, eine neue Welt zu betreten.

L'AUTEUR

Daisann McLane rédige la rubrique du «voyageur frugal» dans les pages «Voyages» du supplément domini-
cal du *New York Times*. Elle contribue également régu-
lièrement au magazine *National Geographic Traveler*,
dans lequel elle tient une colonne. Ses écrits sur les cul-
tures, les cuisines et les musiques du monde sont parus
dans le *Village Voice*, *Vogue* et *Rolling Stone* et elle a
été commentatrice de l'émission *All Things Considered*
de la station NPR. Ses photographies ont été publiées
dans le *New York Times*, *Travel and Leisure* et *Der
Feinschmecker*. Lorsqu'elle ne se trouve pas dans une
chambre d'hôtel bon marché, elle vit à Brooklyn, New
York.

ÉQUIPEMENT

Tous les clichés de cet album ont été pris avec un
Contax Aria 35 mm, équipé d'un objectif 28 mm ou
50 mm Zeiss.

THE AUTHOR

DIE AUTORIN

Daisann McLane writes the Frugal Traveler column for the *New York Times* Sunday travel section, and is a contributing editor and columnist for *National Geographic Traveler* magazine. Her articles on culture, food, and world music have also appeared in the *Village Voice*, *Vogue*, and *Rolling Stone*, and she has been a commentator on NPR's *All Things Considered*. Her photographs have appeared in the *New York Times*, *Travel and Leisure* and *Der Feinschmecker*. When not holed up in cheap hotel rooms, she lives in Brooklyn, New York.

Daisann McLane schreibt die Kolumne „Frugal Traveler" für den Reiseteil in der Sonntagsausgabe der *New York Times* und ist freie Mitarbeiterin und Kolumnistin für die Zeitschrift *National Geographic Traveler*. Ihre Beiträge über Kultur, Essen und Musik sind darüber hinaus in *Village Voice*, *Vogue* und *Rolling Stone* erschienen, und sie war Kommentatorin für *All Things Considered* von NPR. Ihre Fotografien erschienen in der *New York Times*, *Travel and Leisure* und *Der Feinschmecker*. Wenn sie nicht gerade in preiswerten Hotelzimmern haust, lebt sie in Brooklyn, New York.

EQUIPMENT

AUSRÜSTUNG

All of the photos in this book were taken with a Contax Aria 35mm camera, equipped with a 28mm or a 50mm Zeiss lens.

Alle Fotos im Buch wurden mit einer Contax Aria 35 mm Kamera mit 28 mm- und 50 mm-Zeiss-Objektiven aufgenommen.

REMERCIEMENTS

Je remercie mes éditeurs au *New York Times*, Jan Benzel et Nancy Newhouse, qui ont lancé ce projet en 1998 en me suggérant d'acheter un appareil photo et «d'essayer de prendre quelques images de mes chambres d'hôtel». Ursula Mahoney, responsable de la section photo des pages voyages, a été la première à examiner ces clichés (et des milliers d'autres) et à m'encourager à continuer. Mon gourou de la photo, Jim Wolcott, m'a aidée à trouver le bon appareil et les objectifs qui allaient avec, et les équipes de Tamarkin Photo et de Contax USA m'ont permis d'entretenir mon équipement et de le conserver en bon état de marche, des déserts égyptiens à la jungle amazonienne.

Jan et Nancy m'ont également aidée à mettre ce livre au point en m'envoyant faire une présentation devant une classe au Smithsonian Institute. Ne sachant pas comment m'y prendre, j'ai préparé un diaporama de mes photos de chambres d'hôtel accompagné d'un commentaire. Lorsque j'en ai parlé à ma bonne amie Karrie Jacobs, elle a tout de suite vu les possibilités qui m'avaient échappé et m'a immédiatement commandé un article basé sur le même sujet pour son magazine, *dwell*.

Allison Arieff, rédactrice en chef de *dwell*, a eu la perspicacité de voir dans cet article la matière d'un livre et, assistée de Bryan Burkhart, graphiste au talent extraordinaire, a adroitement transformé mes anecdotes et mes images en un superbe projet d'album. Mon infinie gratitude à tous les deux, pour leurs idées, leurs contributions et leurs corrections pendant toutes les phases de la conception de ce livre.

La plupart du temps, j'ai séjourné seule dans les hôtels présentés ici, mais pas toujours. Je souhaite donc remercier également tous les amis et les membres de ma famille qui ont partagé ces chambres bon marché avec moi: Karrie, Enrique, Galen et ma mère, tous de courageux compagnons de voyage.

ACKNOWLEDGEMENTS

DANKSAGUNG

Thanks to my editors at the *New York Times*, Jan Benzel and Nancy Newhouse, who started this project on its way in 1998 when they suggested that I get a camera and "try to take some pictures of my hotel rooms". Ursula Mahoney, the travel section photo editor, was the first person to look at most of these pictures (and thousands more!) and encouraged me to keep going. My camera guru Jim Wolcott helped me find the right camera and lenses to bond with, and the staff at Tamarkin Photo and Contax USA helped me keep the equipment up to date and in good working order, as it flew with me from Egyptian deserts to the Amazon jungle.

Jan and Nancy also helped launch this book by sending me to lecture a class at the Smithsonian Institute; Stumped about what to do, I prepared a slide show of my hotel room pictures, and a commentary. When I told my good friend Karrie Jacobs about this, she saw the potential in it that I did not, and immediately signed me up to do an article based on the material for the magazine that she edits, *dwell*.

Allison Arieff, *dwell*'s senior editor, had the vision to see that article as a book, and deftly turned my anecdotes and pictures into a knockout book proposal, together with Bryan Burkhart, an extraordinarily talented graphic designer. To both, tremendous thanks for your ideas, input, and editing at every stage of this project.

I stayed alone in most of the places that appear here, but occasionally I did not. And so, one last round of thanks to all the friends and family who shared the cheap hotel experience with me: Karrie, Enrique, Galen, and my mom—brave fellow travelers, all.

Dank geht an meine Redakteure bei der *New York Times*, Jan Benzel und Nancy Newhouse, die dieses Projekt 1998 auf den Weg brachten, als sie mir vorschlugen, ich solle eine Kamera mitnehmen und „versuchsweise ein paar Fotos von meinen Hotelzimmern machen". Ursula Mahoney, die Bildredakteurin des Reiseteils, sah sich diese (und Tausende weitere!) Bilder als erste an und ermutigte mich zum Weitermachen. Mein Kameraguru Jim Wolcott unterstützte mich bei der Suche nach der richtigen Kamera und den passenden Objektiven, und die Mitarbeiter bei Tamarkin Photo und Contax USA halfen mir, meine Ausrüstung funktionstüchtig und auf dem neuesten Stand zu halten, solange sie mit mir von der ägyptischen Wüste bis in den Amazonasdschungel reiste.

Der Anstoß zu diesem Buch kam auch wieder von Jan und Nancy, als sie mich zu einem Vortrag vor Studenten des Smithsonian Institute abkommandierten; da mir nichts Besseres einfiel, stellte ich eine Diashow von meinen Hotelzimmer-Fotos zusammen. Als ich meiner guten Freundin Karrie Jacobs davon erzählte, sah sie darin ein Potential, das mir nicht aufgefallen wäre, und beauftragte mich mit einem Artikel für ihre Zeitschrift *dwell*.

Allison Arieff, die Chefredakteurin von *dwell*, hatte den Weitblick, in diesem Artikel das zukünftige Buch zu sehen, und bündelte zusammen mit Bryan Burkhart, einem außerordentlich begabten Grafiker, meine Anekdoten und Fotos zu einem erstklassigen Buch-Exposee. Euch beiden tausend Dank für eure Ideen, euren Input und eure redaktionelle Betreuung in jeder Phase dieses Projekts.

In den meisten hier auftauchenden Häusern bin ich alleine abgestiegen, aber nicht in allen. Darum also eine letzte Runde von Danksagungen an die Freunde und Familienmitglieder, die meine Erfahrungen in preiswerten Hotels mit mir geteilt haben: Karrie, Enrique, Galen und meine Mom – alle wackere Reisegefährten.

A

ARGENTINA (Buenos Aires)

Hotel Castelar
Avenida de Mayo 1152
Tel: (+54-11) 43 83 50 08
Fax: (+54-11) 43 83 83 88
www.castelarhotel.com.ar, $60

B

BAHAMAS (Harbour Island)

Tingum Village International Hotel
P. O. Box 61, Harbour Island
Tel/Fax: (+1242) 333 21 61, $60

BRAZIL (Belem)

Hotel Central
Av. Presidente Vargas 290
Tel: (+55-91) 242 30 11, $19

BRAZIL (Manaus)

SS Nadson Jeane
(enquire at Manaus docks)
1st class passage, $55
Over Look Lodge
c/o Swallows and Amazons Tours
Tel/Fax: (+55-92) 622 12 46
www.swallowsandamazonstours.com, $100
Best Western Manaus
217 Rua Marcilio Dias
Tel: (+55-92) 622 2844
Fax: (+55-92) 622 2576
www.bestwestern.com, $57

BRAZIL (Sao Luís)

Hotel Lord
Rua Nazaré 258
Tel: (+55-98) 221 46 55
Fax: (+55-98) 221 46 74, $40

C

CAMBODIA (Siem Reap)

Golden Apsara Hotel
Mondol 1
No. 220 Khum Svay Dangkum
Tel: (+855-63) 96 35 33
Fax: (+855-63) 38 00 65, $18

CHINA (Hong Kong)

Bishop Lei International House
4 Robinson Road, Mid-Levels
Tel: (+852) 28 68 08 28
Fax: (+852) 28 68 15 51
www.bishopleihtl.com.hk, $75

COOK ISLANDS (Rarotonga)

Aroko Bungalows
P. O. Box 850
Tel: (+682) 236 25, (+682) 216 25
Fax: (+682) 246 25, $45

COOK ISLANDS (Aitutaki)

Maina Sunset Motel
P. O. Box 373, Rarotonga
Tel: (+682) 315 11
Fax: (+682) 316 11
www.soltel.co.ck/maina.htm, $28

CROATIA (Split)

Hotel Bellevue
Josipa Jalacica 2
Tel: (+385-21) 58 57 01
Fax: (+385-21) 36 23 83, $54

D

DOMINICAN REPUBLIC (Las Terrenas)

Casa Robinson
Emilio Prud'homme 2
Tel/Fax: (+1809) 240 64 96, $26

E

EGYPT (Cairo)

Hotel al-Hussein
Khan el-Khalili district
Tel/Fax: (+20-2) 591 84 79, $15

EGYPT (Sinai)

Sanafir Hotel
Naama Bay, Sharm El Sheikh
Tel: (+20-69) 60 01 97
Fax: (+20-69) 60 01 96
www.sanafirhotel.com, $65

APPENDIX

G

GERMANY (Berlin)

Hotel Künstlerheim Luise
Luisenstrasse 19
Tel: (+49-30) 28 44 80,
Fax: (+49-30) 28 44 84 48
www.kuenstlerheim-luise.de, $67

Sorat Art'otel
Joachimstaler Strasse 29
Tel: (+49-30) 88 44 70
Fax: (+49-30) 88 44 77 00
www.sorat-hotels.com, $107

GRENADA (Carriacou)

Bayaleau Point Cottages
Windward
Tel/Fax: (+1473) 443 79 84, $35
www.carriacoucottages.com

I

INDIA (Madras)

Broadlands Lodging House
16 Vallabha Agraham Street
Tel: (+91-44) 854 55 73, $4

INDIA (Kovalam Beach)

Somatheeram Ayurvedic Beach Resort
Chowara, Kerala
Tel: (+91-471) 48 16 01
Fax: (+91-471) 48 06 00
www.somatheeram.com, $65

INDONESIA (Bali)

Candidasa Ghandi Ashram
Candidasa, Karangasem
Tel/Fax: (+62-363) 411 08, $20

Good Karma Bungalows
Selang near Amed, Karangasem
(no telephone), $9

ITALY (Florence)

Hotel Europa
Via Cavour, 14
Tel: (+39-055) 239 67 15,
Fax: (+39-055) 21 03 61
www.webhoteleuropa.com, $82

Hotel Alessandra
Borgo SS. Apostoli, 17
Tel: (+39-055) 28 34 38
Fax: (+39-055) 21 06 19
www.hotelalessandra.com, $87

ITALY (Padova)

Hotel Terme Preistoriche
Via Castello, 5, Montegrotto Terme
Tel: (+39-049) 79 34 77
Fax: (+39-049) 79 36 47
www.termepreistoriche.com, $58

ITALY (Rome)

Hotel Due Torri
Vicolo del Leonetto, 23
Tel: (+39-06) 68 80 69 56
Fax: (+39-06) 68 65 442
www.hotelduetorriroma.com, $87

ITALY (Venice)

Casa Verardo
Castello, 4765
Tel: (+39-041) 528 61 27, $75
www.casaverardo.it

J

JAPAN (Koyasan)

Shojoshin-in Monastery
Bookings through the Koyasan Tourist Association
Tel: (+81-736) 56 26 16
Fax: (+81-736) 56 28 89, $75

JAPAN (Tokyo)

Sawanoya Ryokan
2-3-11 Yanaka
Tel: (+81-3) 38 22 22 51
Fax: (+81-3) 38 22 22 52
www.sawanoya.com, $37

Ryokan Shigetsu
1-31-11 Asakusa
Tel: (+81-3) 38 43 23 45
Fax: (+81-3) 38 43 23 48
www.roy.hi-ho.ne.jp/shigetsu, $55

Hotel Sofitel
2-1-48 Ikenohata
Tel: (+81-3) 56 85 71 11
Fax: (+81-3) 56 85 61 71
www.sofitel.com, $135

K
KOREA (Seoul)
Han Hung Jang Guest House
99 Kwanhun-dong, Jongro-ku
Tel: (+82-2) 734 42 65, $23

KOREA (Sokch'o)
Choksan Hot Spring Resort Village
Tel: (+82-392) 636 40 00
Fax: (+82-392) 636 40 07, $36

L
LAOS (Luang Prabang)
Xieng Mouane Guest House
No. 86/6 Ban Xieng Mouane
Tel/Fax: (+856-71) 25 21 52, $25

LAOS (Vientiane)
Lani 1 Guest House
281 Setthathirat Road
Tel: (+856-21) 21 61 03
Fax: (+856-21) 21 56 39, $30
Le Parasol Blanc Hotel
263 Sibounheuang Road
Tel: (+856-21) 21 60 91
Fax: (+856-21) 22 22 90, $28

M
MALAYSIA (Kuala Lumpur)
Shangri-La
11 Jalan Sultan Ismail
Tel: (+60-3) 20 32 23 88
Fax: (+60-3) 20 70 15 14
www.shangri-la.com, $82

MEXICO (Baja California)
Hotel La Fonda
Km. 59 on the Carrretera Libre Highway
La Fonda, Baja California Norte
(no telephone), $60

N
THE NETHERLANDS (Amsterdam)
Hotel de Filosoof
Anna Vondelstraat 6
Tel: (+31-20) 683 30 13, Fax: (+31-20) 685 37 50
www.hotelfilosoof.nl, $83
Hotel Prinsenhof
Prinsengracht 810
Tel: (+31-20) 623 17 72, Fax: (+31-20) 638 33 68
www.hotelprinsenhof.com, $45

NEW ZEALAND (Auckland)
Peace and Plenty Inn
6 Flagstaff Terrace, Devonport
Tel: (+64-9) 445 29 25, Fax: (+64-9) 445 29 01
www.peaceandplenty.co.nz, $98

P
PANAMA (Bocas del Toro)
La Veranda Hotel
Calle 7, Isla Colón
Tel/Fax: (+507) 757 92 11
www.laverandahotel.com, $35

PANAMA (Boquete)
Hotel Panamonte
Tel: (+507) 720 13 27
Fax: (+507) 720 20 55, $54

PHILIPPINES (Siquijor Island)
Casa de la Playa
Sandugan Beach
Tel: (+63-918) 740 00 79, $13.50

S
SLOVENIA (Lake Bohinj)
Hotel Zlatorog
Ukanc 65, 4265 Bohinjsko Jezero
Tel: (+386-4) 572 33 81, Fax: (+386-4) 572 33 84, $58

SPAIN (Galicia)
Hotel Real
Calderería 49, Santiago de Compostela
Tel: (+34-981) 56 92 90, Fax: (+34-981) 56 92 91
www.hotelreal.com, $44
Doña Maria's House
Village of Camelle
(Go to Bar Chalana and enquire with bartender), $11

Hostal Gaviota
Calle del Rio 15, Camariñas
Tel: (+34-981) 73 65 22, $15

SPAIN (Canary Islands)
Casa La Punta
Hermigua, La Gomera
Rented through Ecotural La Gomera
Tel/Fax: (+34-922) 14 41 01
www.ecoturismocanarias.com/gomera, $42

SPAIN (Madrid)
Hotel París
Puerta del Sol, Calle Alcalá, 2
Tel: (+34-91) 521 64 96
Fax: (+34-91) 531 01 88, $55
Hostal Rifer
Calle Mayor 5
Tel/Fax: (+34-91) 532 31 97, $26

T
THAILAND (Bangkok)
Peachy Guest House
10 Phra Athit Road, Banglamphu
Tel: (+66-2) 281 64 71, $12.50

TONGA (Ha'apai)
Fifita Guest House
Tel: (+676) 602 13, $7.50

TONGA (Vava'u)
The Tongan Beach Resort
P. O. Box 104, Neiafu
Tel/Fax: (+676) 703 80
www.thetongan.com, $70

U
UNITED STATES
CALIFORNIA (Big Sur)
Deetjen's Big Sur Inn
48865 Highway 1, Big Sur
Tel: (+1-831) 667 23 77
Fax: (+1-831) 667 04 66
www.deetjens.com, $125

CALIFORNIA (Los Angeles)
Bevonshire Lodge Motel
7575 Beverly Boulevard
Tel: (+1-323) 936 61 54, Fax: (+1-323) 934 66 40, $45

CALIFORNIA (Napa Valley)
White Sulphur Springs Resort and Spa
3100 White Sulphur Springs Road, St. Helena
Tel: (+1-707) 963 85 88, Fax: (+1-707) 963 28 90
www.whitesulphursprings.com, $185 / four person cabin

CALIFORNIA (Ojai)
Capri Motel
1180 East Ojai Avenue
Tel: (+1-877) 589 58 60
www.caprimotel.com, $79

CALIFORNIA (Paso Robles)
Paso Robles Inn
1103 Spring Street
Tel: (+1-805) 238 26 60, Fax: (+1-805) 238 47 07
www.pasoroblesinn.com, $112

CALIFORNIA (San Francisco)
Marina Inn
3110 Octavia at Lombard
Tel: (+1-415) 928 10 00
Fax: (+1-415) 928 59 09
www.marinainn.com, $67.50
The Andrews Hotel
624 Post Street
Tel: (+1-415) 563 68 77
Fax: (+1-415) 928 69 19
www.andrewshotel.com, $85
Hotel del Sol
3100 Webster Street
Tel: (+1-415) 921 55 20
Fax: (+1-415) 931 41 37
www.thehoteldelsol.com, $99

DISTRICT OF COLUMBIA (Washington)
Hotel George
15 E Street NW
Tel: (+1-202) 347 42 00
Fax: (+1-202) 347 42 13
www.hotelgeorge.com, $129

Tabard Inn
1739 N Street NW
Tel: (+1-202) 785 12 77
www.tabardinn.com, $75

FLORIDA (Big Pine Key)
The Barnacle Bed and Breakfast
1557 Long Beach Drive
Tel: (+1-305) 872 32 98
Fax: (+1-305) 872 38 63, $115
www.thebarnacle.net
Deer Run Bed and Breakfast
1997 Long Beach Road
Tel: (+1-305) 872 20 15
Fax: (+1-305) 515 02 08, $95

HAWAII (Honolulu)
Ohana Edgewater
2168 Kalia Road
Tel: (+1-808) 922 19 64
Fax: (+1-808) 923 46 32, $69
Aston at the Executive Centre Hotel
1088 Bishop Street
Tel: (+1-808) 539 30 00
Fax: (+1-808) 523 10 88
www.astonexecutive.com, $128

ILLINOIS (Chicago)
Motel 6
(now Red Roof Inn)
162 East Ontario Street
Tel: (+1-312) 78 73 580
Fax: (+1-312) 78 71 299
www.redroof.com, $102
Park Brompton Inn
(now renamed Majestic Hotel)
528 West Brompton Avenue
Tel: (+1-773) 404 34 99
Fax: (+1-773) 404 34 95, $125

MINNESOTA (Grand Marais)
Rockwood Lodge and Canoe Outfitters
50 Rockwood Road, Gunflint Trail
Tel: (+1-218) 388 22 42
Fax: (+1-240) 526 55 64, $40

NEW YORK (Manhattan)
On The Ave Hotel
2178 Broadway
Tel: (+1-212) 362 11 00
Fax: (+1-212) 787 95 21
www.ontheave.com, $125
Hotel Wolcott
4 West 31st Street
Tel: (+1-212) 268 29 00
Fax: (+1-212) 563 00 96
www.wolcott.com, $99
The New Yorker Hotel
481 Eighth Avenue
Tel: (+1-212) 971 01 01
Fax: (+1-212) 629 65 36
www.hotelnewyorker.com, $99

PENNSYLVANIA (Philadelphia)
Shippen Way Inn
416-18 Bainbridge Street
Tel: (+1-215) 627 72 66
Fax: (+1-215) 627 77 81, $99

TEXAS (San Antonio)
The Painted Lady Inn
620 Broadway
Tel: (+1-210) 220 10 92
Fax: (+1-210) 299 41 85
www.thepaintedladyinn.com, $99
Adams House Bed and Breakfast Inn
231 Adams Street
Tel: (+1-210) 224 47 91
www.adams-house.com, $89

TEXAS (Houston)
Robin's Nest Bed and Breakfast
4104 Greeley Street
Tel: (+1-713) 528 58 21
Fax: (+1-713) 521 21 54, $99

We recommend that you call to verify addresses and other information. Prices listed subject to change.

Bo. Nov. 05

404

17·25 (19·25) 27385